I'M
STILL
HUNGRY

ALSO BY CARNIE WILSON

Gut Feelings:
From Fear and Despair to Health and Hope

★

OTHER HAY HOUSE
TITLES OF RELATED INTEREST

Books

Losing Your Pounds of Pain: *Breaking the Link Between Abuse,
Stress, and Overeating,* by Doreen Virtue, Ph.D.

The Power Is Within You, by Louise L. Hay

Shape® Magazine's Shape Your Life:
4 Weeks to a Better Body—and a Better Life,
by Barbara Harris, Editor-in-Chief, *Shape*® magazine, with Angela Hynes

The TOPS Way to Weight Loss: *Beyond Calories and Exercise,*
by Howard Rankin, Ph.D. (available January 2004)

The Truth: *The Only Fitness Book You'll Ever Need,*
by Frank Sepe (available January 2004)

A Very Hungry Girl:
How I Filled Up on Life . . . And How You Can, Too!
by Jessica Weiner (available January 2004)

The Yo-Yo Diet Syndrome: *How to Heal and Stabilize Your
Appetite and Weight,* by Doreen Virtue, Ph.D.

Card Decks

Healthy Body Cards, by Louise L. Hay

Juicy Living Cards, by SARK (available October 2003)

Self-Care Cards, by Cheryl Richardson

All of the above are available at your local bookstore,
or may be ordered through Hay House, Inc.:

(800) 654-5126 or **(760) 431-7695**
(800) 650-5115 (fax) or **(760) 431-6948 (fax)**
www.hayhouse.com

I'M
STILL
HUNGRY

Finding Myself
Through Thick and Thin

Carnie Wilson
with Cindy Pearlman

HAY
HOUSE

Hay House, Inc.
Carlsbad, California • Sydney, Australia • London, U.K.
Canada • Hong Kong

Published and distributed in the United States by: Hay House, Inc., P.O. Box 5100, Carlsbad, CA 92018-5100 • **Phone:** (760) 431-7695 or (800) 654-5126 • **Fax:** (760) 431-6948 or (800) 650-5115 • www.hayhouse.com • **Published and distributed in Australia by:** Hay House Australia Ltd., 18/36 Ralph St., Alexandria NSW 2015 • **Phone:** 612-9669-4299 • **Fax:** 612-9669-4144 • www.hayhouse.com.au • **Published and Distributed in the United Kingdom by:** Hay House UK, Ltd. • Unit 202, Canalot Studios • 222 Kensal Rd., London W10 5BN • **Phone:** 44-20-8962-1230 • **Fax:** 44-20-8962-1239 • www.hayhouse.co.uk • **Distributed in Canada by:** Raincoast • 9050 Shaughnessy St., Vancouver, B.C. V6P 6E5 • **Phone:** (604) 323-7100 • **Fax:** (604) 323-2600

Editorial supervision: Jill Kramer   *Design:* Amy Rose Szalkiewicz
Interior photos: Greg Bertolini

Library of Congress Cataloging-in-Publication Data

Wilson, Carnie
  I'm still hungry : finding myself through thick and thin / Carnie Wilson, with Cindy Pearlman.
      p. cm.
  ISBN 1-4019-0227-8 (Hardcover) — ISBN 1-4019-0228-6 (Tradepaper) 1. Wilson, Carnie, 1968—Health.
      2. Overweight women—United States—Biography. 3. Jejunoileal bypass–Patients—United States–Biography.
      4. Women singers—United States—Biography. I. Pearlman, Cindy, 1964- II. Title.
  RC628.W526 2003
  362.1'96398'0092—dc21

                                         2003004570

                          Hardcover ISBN 1-4019-0227-8
                          Tradepaper ISBN 1-4019-0228-6

                          06 05 04 03   5 4 3 2
                               1st printing, June 2003
                               2nd printing, June 2003

                    Printed in the United States of America

★

This book is dedicated to the person who invented the old-fashioned glazed buttermilk doughnut. I could ring your neck, because I'll always be tortured by the thought of eating one. But I could also give you a hug for all the times I ate three at once and couldn't believe something could taste that good. You are part of the reason I needed gastric-bypass surgery. Ha-ha!

Okay, for real: This book is for all the people who have ever struggled with a weight problem or some type of addiction. Only you know what it's like. But my message is that you <u>can</u> change something about yourself if you really want to. The power belongs to you.

★

❂ Contents

Preface

The other night I had a really weird, but delicious, dream. In a long, flowing white gown and bare feet, I was running through soft, ticklish grass toward a secret garden. Breathing deeply, I stepped inside, blinked, and noticed something strange about the Technicolor landscape. I was sinking, but not into soil—the dark dirt turned out to be a super-rich fudge-brownie mix. Hoisting myself out of this high-fat quicksand, I found a stony path; yet the "rock" was actually wet walnuts stuck together with a substance so foreign to me that I stifled a scream. It was real butter! Ditching the path, I ran wildly through a field, where something was suddenly poking at my feet. It wasn't the tips of grass blades, but an endless carpet of rainbow-colored sprinkles.

"Why is this happening? I hardly ever eat dessert anymore!" I cried as I fell down and grasped at the stem of a sunflower to stand up. But just as quickly, I pulled my hand back in horror to realize it wasn't a plant I was clutching, but a gigantic chocolate biscotti. At this point, I knew that if I could just make it to the shimmering pond in the distance, I could stop and catch my breath. As I came closer, however, I noticed that it wasn't a body of water at all, but moving waves of thick hot fudge with a crunchy crème brûlée island in the middle.

All I could do at this point was pray to a higher power. "Lord, help me," I whispered as I looked up at the sky, but those weren't regular clouds up there. It was all marshmallow fluff.

Suddenly, I bolted up in bed, gazed at my sleeping husband and our three dogs, and understood that those last pulse-racing moments had just been a nightmare. In the quiet darkness, I also realized something else: *Fuck, I'm _still_ hungry.*

I know that's not what you were expecting from my new book. Admit it, you were waiting for me to say that I found inner peace eating a tofu burger, happiness in a pair of size-six jeans, and the true meaning of life when I made eye contact with my ankles again.

Of course, all of the above is true, and we'll get to that part in a bit. But let's begin this book by being honest: I've lost more than 150 pounds, and you bet my now-thinner ass that I'm still hungry. Yes, I'm still hungry for buttermilk doughnuts, but that's not what I'm really talking about here. After life-saving weight-loss surgery (WLS) and keeping the pounds off for more than three years, let me tell you that I'm hungry for more: more knowledge, more truth, more connections, and more satisfaction in my life. The flip side is that I'm full these days in ways that have nothing to do with food, while I'm also satisfied after a meal for the first time in my life.

Even I can't believe it. Of course, my eyes are still bigger than my gut . . . speaking of which, my journey began in my first book, *Gut Feelings,* where I took you through my childhood and years of being the fat chick both in private and in the public eye—including singing with Wilson Phillips and hosting my own daily talk show. I also told the story of how I met and married the love of my life, Rob. In addition, I talked about having gastric-bypass surgery and finally finding the guts to prove to myself that with enough effort, determination, and willpower (a word that didn't exist in my dictionary a few years ago), you really can change your life.

That dream came true . . . but there was more to come.

So let's dig in.

✪ ✪ ✪

✪ Acknowledgments

There are so many people I wish I had the space to thank. This book is an accumulation of people and experiences that have touched me and made a difference in my life—I hope it's been symbiotic!

First, I'd like to thank Cindy Pearlman, who wrote this book with me. I loved you from the moment we met, and I just want you to know that you did a beautiful job. Our minds and our spirits are alike, which is why the book came together like this. You're gifted and talented, not to mention a total sweetheart.

Special thanks go to:

Hay House, for giving me another opportunity to touch more lives.

Danny Levin, for your big heart and for suggesting Cindy as my collaborator.

Jill Kramer and Shannon Littrell—your input was amazing. Thank you for everything.

Spotlighthealth.com—we continue to provide hope, offer important information, and educate people who need us desperately.

Dr. Alan Wittgrove for his magical skill, and to Dr. Steven Zax for his experience and gentleness, and for my great set of tits (okay, okay—*breasts*).

Leslie Jester, who will always have my respect, trust, loyalty, and heart.

Wilson Phillips for never fading.

The William Morris Agency voice-over department—you're all wonderful.

Blockbuster for giving me the hamster-and-rabbit campaign.

The folks at Doner—Ron Rose and Davis Glick—for all the fun we've had.

Al Jardine, I'll never forget our memories together. And I'll be forever grateful because through you I met my husband.

Marilyn Grabowski and Steve Wayda at *Playboy* for believing in me and making me feel beautiful.

Marc Schoen for helping me grow and feel safer.

Daniel and Brian for your generosity and our laughter.

Pam Miller for your friendship, patience, and invaluable guidance.

Tiffany for taking the plunge and joining me. Now we can do it together.

Mickey Shapiro, my friend and manager—without you, I would not be who I am or where I am today. We share many things together and work our butts off for what you and I dream of—balance, love, and success. This is our time. I love you.

My wonderful family and dear friends—there are just too many to mention, but you know I love you very much.

My sweet, loving sister, Wendy, whom I admire and who lives her life with great integrity.

Dad, Melinda, and Gloria for being so strong.

My stepfather, Daniel, for loving Mom and making her laugh every day.

My mother, Marilyn, for always doing the right thing, for teaching me to be real, and for her special love that's always beaming in my heart.

My husband, Rob, the man I decided to share my life with—thank you for being my special best friend, my lover, and my other half. You are an angel sent to me. I love you, darling. I love that face.

An extra big (no pun intended!) acknowledgment to gastric-bypass patients—we're brave, and we'll always share the connection.

Oh, I can't forget our dogs, Willie, Olive, and Sammy. Who could live without that kind of love?

And extra special thanks to Aney (Katrina), my quiet little editor. I love and appreciate you.

✪ ✪ ✪

✪ Introduction

One . . . Five . . . Zero

For starters, I'd like to introduce you to the half of me that recently came to life. You've actually never met her before because she was, well, let's just say "undercover" for many years.

My name is Carnie Wilson. Did I mention that I lost 150 pounds? (High five!) One . . . five . . . zero. Thank God, I lost just about everything except my sense of humor. That's why I wanted to call this book *Fuck, I'm Still Hungry*. Except I was told that the title would cause some people in the Bible Belt to actually pass out, which is never a good thing. Oh, and I was also informed that some big chain stores (you know who you are) wouldn't carry the book. What to do? Along the way, *Survival of the Fattest* was also turned down. (Funny or too out there? Your call.) Personally, I liked *Running with Twinkies,* but frankly, I can't imagine how we'd do product tie-ins: "But she only eats *part* of the low-fat cream filling!"

I adored this subtitle: *Dealing with Success, Attaining a Goal, Then Trying to Sabotage the Shit Out of It!* You see, I'm sure you think that after I had weight-loss surgery (WLS) and lost all those pounds, my life would be totally perfect—the end. Actually, it was just the beginning.

When I decided to have WLS, I made a conscious and quite serious decision to change myself on the outside. But I also had to change how I felt on the inside, to cope with the scars that no one else could see, but that *I* could feel down to my marrow. These wounds lurked deep inside of me, as if they'd been waiting all my life for me to lose the weight and find them underneath all that protective gear. Another great title for this book could have been *Still an Onion,* because I feel as if I'm still peeling away all my layers.

Frankly, it was almost a no-brainer to decide to have the surgery. That little voice inside of me said, "If you don't do this, Carnie, then you're going to die. You'll cease to exist on this planet." When I ignored this voice, it would remind me, "You need to realize that you're the only one who can save your own life. Your mom or dad can't make you do it, your sister can't tell you to do it—*you* have to do it for yourself." When I shed the weight, the voice started piping up again (damn it!). This time it said, "So you saved your life. Now what?"

Leslie Jester, a special friend of mine who's also a nurse, told me that my surgery would be only 25 percent physical—75 percent of it would be emotional. At first, I didn't believe her. After my surgery, I thought, *Ohhh, it's gonna be so incredible. I'll lose all the weight, buy a bikini, feel so good, and everything will be okay.* How many of us have said over and over again: "If I just lose the weight, then my life will be perfect"? Or we take it one step further: "I'll lose the weight, get a great job, meet the perfect guy, make a million dollars, and get up every morning next to my husband, Brad Pitt, only to say, 'Wow, I wonder if we should go to a premiere tonight or just stay at home and have hours of mind-blowing sex?'"

I know it looks a bit ridiculous in print—especially the part about Brad Pitt. (Feel free to substitute Colin Farrell if you want.) Seriously, I think that we numb ourselves with these easy solutions because it's a way to avoid paying attention to what we're really feeling.

Well, my physical transformation definitely happened. I was reborn—and freed from an all-you-can-eat prison. Then I had to open my eyes and really wake up. I realized that I'd chosen to give myself a second chance . . . now I had to decide what to do with it.

Losing the weight didn't mean getting rid of my emotional issues. In fact, I'd previously used my fat as a sort of barrier—it was my way of never letting anyone see how much pain I was in. Over the years, I'd accumulated a lot of baggage from stress, fear, insecurity, failures, disappointments, and other things I call "the bad stuff." After losing half of myself, I had to find a way to purge all that stuff, *and* I had to change the way I felt about myself. It didn't matter that 150 pounds were off my bod—I still had the same problems in that one area where it's really difficult to tone things up: my brain.

My weight loss was just the starting point—if I wanted to be an unhealthy thin person, then I could continue making decisions that made me feel bad and caused me to gain the weight in the first place. My therapist, Marc, and I talk about this all the time. Even when I was fat, I longed to feel safe and comforted. Yes, I can be a very outgoing girl, but sometimes that's just a cover-up.

In the past, I didn't feel secure, so I made myself feel better by overeating. Now I really can't eat like that anymore, so I have to work very hard to get my feelings in check. If I don't get the emotional part down, I could very well still snack myself back to a size 20 (or beyond).

So I decided that if I wanted to be a *together* thin person, then I'd also have to shed my emotional bad habits. This, believe it or not, was a far tougher task than getting rid of the pounds. For starters, it's a bit more tricky to measure this progress. I couldn't exactly step on a scale to see how much emotional baggage I'd lost; instead, I charted my success by the smile on my face when I woke up in the morning and the calm feeling I had when I closed my eyes at night. I had to take a different type of load off to get there—and some days were certainly better than others. On the plus side, I bet I've burned off an awful lot of calories getting to this place. After all, if vacuuming burns 100 calories an hour, then soul-searching must be worth at least as much (maybe more!).

In the process, I've found this new person who knows what it's like to finally feel free and more confident—but I still have the emotional triggers, the sad days, and the moments when I just want to sit down and cry. And that's exactly what I do. (Damn, it feels good.) In other words, this isn't one of those books where I'll just say, "I lost the weight, and now I get up in the morning, hug a tree, and my life is great." If only it were that simple. If only *I* were that simple. Never have been, never will be.

✪

When I'm searching for answers, I know I must go back to the beginning. My weight problem started around age four or five in the fabulous disco '70s when I began to boogie to the fridge for lots of snacks. Let's just say that when I talked about "Little Debbie," I didn't mean the kid down the street.

When I was eight, I remember that Dad—the awesomely talented Brian Wilson of The Beach Boys—was around 311 pounds because he loved to eat ice cream and birthday cake for dinner. But really, who wouldn't? Forget the pot roast and salad—pass the mint chocolate-chip ice cream and baked goods (and I'll have a second helping, thank you very much). My mom also struggled with her weight. In our house, we ate a lot of kugel, which is basically noodles, sugar, more noodles, more sugar, and you can add raisins if the thing just isn't sweet enough. It was fabulous. But there were also things at home that weren't so good way back when. . . .

As a kid, I couldn't begin to understand why my family wasn't like those people down the block who ate dinner together every night and went on family vacations during the summer. Yet I did know that I had something special that the other kids weren't exposed to. At a very young age, I realized that I was truly moved by music and extremely sensitive to people's vibes and energy, like my father. When I was a kid, I would have done anything for Dad's attention, and food seemed to be something we had in common. Other kids tossed the ball around with their pop; my dad and I shared "The Zoo" at Shakey's Pizza—a 30-scoop ice-cream dish (yum!). If you can believe it, we'd actually finish the entire thing!

Sugar was my constant companion as a kid, and it's easy to figure out why: It just made me feel so good. What didn't make me feel so great were the watchful eyes of my parents, who were obviously worried because I was growing and growing and growing. My sister, Wendy, kept growing taller, while I kept growing sideways. I was 110 pounds by the fourth grade; 200 pounds at the end of high school; and by age 30, I saw 300 on the scale. It got to the point that I couldn't even walk around anymore, which scared me. And at night, I'd often wake up gasping for air because I had something called *sleep apnea,* which meant that my fat was actually choking me to death.

My body was a combat zone—my organs versus my fat. I knew that if I stayed 300 pounds, I might make it through a few more battles, but I'd definitely lose the war. In my mind's eye, I could see that night when I'd be struggling to breathe and wouldn't be able to find enough to satisfy my lungs. I even had visions that my mother would get a terrifying call in the middle of the night from me. I'd barely be able to talk, but she'd know I was in trouble. My sad home movie ended with Mom and Wendy arriving to find my dead body.

What also scared the shit out of me was when my doctor diagnosed me with the deadly disease called *obesity,* which he said would eventually kill me. I was already pre-diabetic, my cholesterol and blood pressure were dangerously high, and my gallbladder was starting to produce stones. I had slipped discs in my back, chronic headaches, joint pain, and asthma. Yet I still managed to have pancakes and bacon for breakfast, and a Big Mac and a 20-piece Chicken McNuggets with fries for lunch—I was like everyone else who lives with one foot in a big vat of denial.

One morning, however, I could no longer deny my condition. I looked in the mirror and noticed that I had temporary paralysis in my face (or Bell's palsy). Suddenly, being the funny fat girl was no longer so funny.

Now I realize that God was putting my life on freeze-frame and giving me the ultimate wake-up call: *LOSE WEIGHT NOW!* I knew that I had to do something dramatic to force myself to change, and that happened on August 10, 1999, when I had gastric-bypass surgery and decided to save my life. I like to call it my own personal 911. In other words, I came to my own rescue.

These days when people tell me, "I don't know what to do anymore," I only have one answer for them, and it's quite simple: "You have to save yourself."

★

To answer the question of why I've written another book, we need to make a quick trek to the past again. I remember when we were children, Wendy and I were playing the board game Candy Land, and she was beating me. I stomped around the room until my mother took me out into the hallway. "Honey, you have to learn how to be a good loser," she said. Of course, I gave her my sweetest, apple-cheeked smile and a quick peck on the cheek before making my return to the bedroom, where I promptly pinched Wendy as hard as possible. Her yowl could be heard several states away. Let me just say that I was never a good loser, and I'm sorry, Wen. (Although if Mom's reading this, I still deny it ever happened.)

Anyway, this got me thinking about losing half of my former self. Am I being a good loser now? Maybe you'll understand what I mean by the end of this book.

I *am* proud that I've happily lost a certain part of my negativity, yet haven't lost the ability to revel in the absurd. The other day, my husband, Rob, and I took out my pair of size-28 jeans, which in the old days fit sort of tight after a meal. Did he say, "Oh, honey, I'm so proud of you"? Did I say, "Look at how far I've come, baby"? No. I said (and I quote myself exactly here), "Wow! I really had a fat ass back then!"

To which Rob said what any husband on this earth knows are the only words allowed to guarantee his survival: "Honey, you're crazy!"

I hugged him with arms that I still wish were more toned, but they're getting there.

The whole purpose of *I'm Still Hungry* is to inspire other people and open their eyes when it comes to making a major life change, whatever it may be. Of course, I know some of you are thinking, *I don't care about all of this emotional crap. Let's just get to the weight-loss stuff so that I can take off a quick five pounds.*

Well, I've got you covered in the next chapter, which I decided to put at the very front of the book. Here, I'll tell you a few things I've discovered when it comes to the neurotic, pathetic excuses we use in the name of "dieting." (I know you'll probably relate—especially when I get to the part about weighing myself in the nude.)

Moving along, Part I talks about how I shaped my body, while Part II focuses on how I toned up my mind. And finally, the book's Appendix includes even more weight-loss tips, including how to follow my diet, which will work whether you've had WLS or not. There's even a special section for those who want to have gastric-bypass surgery. Wait a sec, now you're probably saying, "Where the hell is all that sexy stuff about *Playboy?*" Feel free to skip ahead to Chapter 15. I would.

I'm assuming that's what my favorite flight attendant might do as well. It's strange how the most casual observer can put it all in perspective when you least expect it. "Carnie Wilson!" said Roxanne Hott, who at 30,000 feet over the Grand Canyon was carefully pouring my coffee as I recently winged home from visiting a hospital. She informed me that I could call her by her nickname, "Hot Roxy" (I didn't ask).

"It's so nice to meet you, hon," she said, offering me some creamer for my coffee and then shaking her head. "Girl, you've really been through it all—thick and thin," she said.

"Hot Roxy, don't I know it," I said. (Thanks for helping with the title of this book, you doll!)

On this journey through thick and thin, I realize that I may have lost the equivalency of one person, but I've gained a whole new one. I found her hiding under those protective layers of fat, and she's still five years old and scared. That's the part that I still need to work on. That's the real deal.

Does the new me still crave buttermilk pancakes with tons of maple syrup? Ohhhhh, yes!

Do I eat them? Hell, no! I'm not that hungry—believe it or not.

✪ ✪ ✪

❂ Friendly Food Facts for You

Let's cut to the chase already. I know that by now you're probably thinking, *Jeez, Carn, I know you went through a lot and had your drastic surgery, but I'd like one frickin' weight-loss tip before we get started with this 200-page book!*

Well, hang on a second, because I just dropped half a cup of shredded mozzarella cheese into my one egg for breakfast, and I think a grease fire might be starting soon. I really should start measuring the cheese . . . or perhaps I've invented something that chef Emeril Lagasse might devote a show to—flaming cheese egg. *Bam!* Love him!

To be honest, if I'm being good, my day will start off with just this dish and a little teaspoon of ketchup. If I'm feeling a little more like a fiesta mama—like Maria Carmen Lupe Rosita Margarita Sanchez, my alter ego (I love doing a Spanish accent!)—I might stick the egg dish in a flour tortilla, but I probably should skip the carbs. And that's the first food tip of this book!

All right, since I've spent many years compiling a list of common dieting myths and misconceptions, I've decided to tell you the truth about a few things. For instance, as I mentioned above, you really *should* measure shredded cheese. Many of us are guilty of skipping this step, even though if we took the time to tape it together, all that cheese we're using would stretch from California to New York. In other words, that's not 110 calories.

Also, in a perfect world, I would honestly believe in the concept of Entenmann's Light, but my rational mind screams, "There's nothing light about something called 'fudge coconut twists'!"

It's time to face the facts when it comes to food fantasies. I've learned the hard way that we must confront a buffet of hard truths:

1. Eating food out of the garbage is not only gross, but those calories do count. It's just another way the universe makes life difficult for women and hungry sanitation workers (eww! You never know!). For instance, I've thrown away the last half of a pound cake I served friends, yet I kept thinking about it sitting in the trash. I tried to convince myself that it was next to the gunk from the vacuum-cleaner bags and the old coffee grinds, but I knew in my heart that I'd secretly placed that pound cake in the totally hygienic spot between two completely clean magazines, so no harm done, right?

Wrong. Yes, the garbage cake is a little gross and mushy from exposure, heat, and moisture condensation, but it still contains butter, eggs, flour, and sugar. In other words, if you perform an emergency save from the trash, the calories will still count. If you stand at the trash can like my new best friend, Miranda from *Sex and the City* (remember that episode where she's having foreplay with a Betty Crocker cake that she tossed in the garbage?), it still counts. So now when I pass a Hefty bag, I remind myself that my dog Willie's throw up was in there last week, too. Eww, vile!

2. A pair of Victoria's Secret underwear weighs approx-imately five ounces. For the purposes of historical accuracy and to satisfy the Federal Agency that Measures Undies (FAMU), I weighed my best black ones on my professional food scale. Let's get real: Taking off those undies before you weigh yourself ain't gonna do shit. It will just be a little cold and drafty when you stand on the scale (which, of course, you might enjoy). Let me also state for the record that despite the facts listed above, I never, ever, wear my white panties with the extra lace when I weigh myself because God only knows that all that lace is why I'm up a pound. I mean, it's really, *really* heavy lace. . . .

3. On an incredibly foul note, you might not think that a big poop makes a difference, but it does. Enough said. I can't believe I just wrote that, but we all know it's true. Weighing myself after I take a poop counts because, unlike my underwear, I have no idea how much certain waste material weighs, and my food scale is *not* getting involved. Okay, I'm done.

4. Speaking of the scale, I've found that moving it to the place in the bathroom where the floor naturally dips won't reflect my accurate weight, but it will point out a defect in the construc-tion of my house. Also, getting on the scale while leaning like that tower in Pisa isn't good (although if I ever write a yoga book, I guarantee that I'll invent a few new poses that can be done in any bathroom in America). And, if you slightly touch the countertop with two fingers, lifting yourself up just a bit, well, that's no good either. (Holding on to the counter after reading the number on the scale, however, is perfectly understandable due to shock.)

5. As for health-food stores, just because their licorice is all natural and comes from that field in Austria where the horses run free and Julie Andrews is singing in the hills . . . well, it's still freaking candy! I don't really shop that much at those places because part of the excitement of candy buying for me comes from seeing the M&Ms logo—and I want to know that my Snickers is really Snickers. When I have my desperate moments, the more expensive organic chocolate doesn't have any fewer calories than a plain-brown wrapper that reads: Hershey's. Sorry to break the bad news—although those pastures on the wrappers of your organic chocolate sure are pretty.

6. Those sugar-free candies? You know, the ones with the fabulous chemical sweeteners that we can't even pronounce? Let me just say that there better be a bathroom nearby, or prepare for a series of farts that seem like you invented a new scent: Eau de Hell. It's not worth it.

7. It's true that a Mt. Everest-sized scoop of light sour cream isn't really so light, especially when you use a soup ladle to smother it all over everything. While we're on the topic, let me address those so-called low-fat cookies that legally I can't mention but that rhyme with "Whack Swells." I know I can't just eat one or two (even though I don't really like them because they taste fake and full of chemicals anyway), but did you ever look at how high the sugar content is in these low-fat products? Just go for that one real cookie (or only eat half), and then revel in the happy memory of the chips, the cinnamon, the crispiness . . . okay, you get the picture. I'll stop obsessing.

8. Frosting truly is the devil. Baking something for your loved one just so *you* can eat the rest of the frosting out of the can when no one's looking—well, I think we could easily do a whole hour on *Oprah* about that. Until that happens, I'll just say that you should keep your fingers off those dangerous, make-it-easy-for-you, bastard pull-tabs.

9. Batter is just uncooked food. When you really think about it, you're eating raw eggs, which is really scary. Remember in the movie *Rocky* when he slurped raw eggs? That always freaked me out. I mean, would you ever open the fridge door, crack an egg, and eat it? Just think about that every time you want to scrape the bowl with your finger—unless you're Martha Stewart and you have your own chickens, but how unrealistic is that concept? With batter, convince yourself that if you eat it, you might die from some weird bacteria that I think may have killed several plump (although happy) chefs in Europe.

10. You can't always blame your weight on being bloated. After all, ten pounds didn't suddenly appear because: (a) You're going to get your period; (b) you just got your period; or (c) in 29 days, you'll be getting your annoying, bloat-causing, period again.

11. Low-calorie hot fudge? Stop the madness!

12. The easiest and most exciting weight-loss method I've tried is chewing food and then spitting it out. This way, you get the taste and the experience of chewing the food, without all of the fat and calories (although you'll still get some). Now this is really not attractive on dates—when you run to the bathroom, he might think you're bulimic. Worst of all, your own mother might slap you on the hand even if you're 35 years old, because those aren't exactly the table manners she taught you. But once in a while, when you just need to *taste* that piece of chocolate, it's better than eating it. And when you do spit it in the garbage, make sure to aim for that leftover pound cake you're supposedly avoiding.

13. Diets? They're the biggest weight-loss myth of all, and eventually part of the reason I had gastric-bypass surgery. Read on.

✪ ✪ ✪

Part I

The Big Loser
(Congratulations!)

• Introduction to Part I

Anyone who loves food can attest to the fact that the middle is always the best part—just look at Tootsie Pops, Oreo cookies, and Hostess Twinkies (don't even get me started on that cream filling).

The same holds true for my battle with weight—the middle part of my journey from fat girl to thin woman is by far the most interesting. I'm talking about when I was actually losing the weight. After all, I didn't go from A to Z in the blink of an eye.

So, what follows is my path through the first two years of my weight loss, with all of the triumphs, challenges, and disappointments I encountered along the way. I also discovered the miracle of being able to avoid saying the following: "Screw this, I want my Snickers *and* my fried chicken."

Like so many of you, I've been through countless diets that didn't work. But until now, I've never been on the other end of the struggle—where I've actually whipped this thing called *obesity.*

In this part of the book, I'm going to provide a weight-loss diary of sorts, so I can tell you exactly how I did it . . . because it wasn't easy. I've also provided a "poundage time line," which will help you see how I made it down to the next level while struggling with all of the emotional issues that could have stopped my progress and returned me to those size-28 jeans.

Sure, I had surgery, but I could have easily gone back to my old ways without losing a single pound. Oh my God—could you even imagine? Well, don't worry. I *did* lose the weight, and this is exactly how I did it.

✪ ✪ ✪

chapter One

The Incredible Shrinking Woman

<u>August to October 1999</u>

- ✪ *Weight on the day of my surgery:* 289
- ✪ *Weight at the end of October:* 214
- ✪ *Sizes:* from 28 to 18

Let's begin with the math. Before my surgery, I stepped on the scale and it registered 298 pounds, which was obviously horrific. I think my heart might have stopped, because I knew that someone seeing that kind of number on a scale at 31 years old wouldn't live to see 90 (or even 40). It was a sad but simple truth that I was going to die young, and I had to do something to stop this from happening.

During the time I was prepping for my surgery, I actually dropped down to 289 pounds without doing much of anything except worrying, so let's credit my overly active nervous system for that helpful nudge in the right direction. We've all been on the High-Anxiety Weight-Loss Plan—when we've been dumped, gotten fired, or experienced any other upsetting life event. Somehow our metabolism kicks in like we've just done three hours on the treadmill. No one needs to be on this plan, no matter how effective it might be.

Anyway, on August 10, 1999, I saved my life.

When I woke up after surgery, I thanked God for allowing me to get through the operation . . . and then I dozed off again after hitting my morphine button a few times. In my conscious moments, I noticed that my entire body either hurt or felt numb. As grateful as I was, I was also a mess. I couldn't turn over with all the tubes attached to me, and I also ached for simple pleasures such as being able to sleep on my stomach again (which was out of the question for a good month).

I needed 11 pillows to find any sort of comfort. Even though my mom kept rearranging them, I never did find relief. Mom was a saint who took care of me right after surgery. I was a big baby, and she went *way* beyond the call of duty—she not only wiped away my tears, but she also wiped . . . you know what? Let's stop right here. Only a mother would do these things.

As for eating, my post-op consisted of delicious ice chips followed by water. The next day I had my first meal, which was a few sips of chicken broth and some Jell-O. Rosemary, my nurse, made everything pleasant and exciting. I loved her.

Not to get too medical on anyone, but my tummy pouch was now the size of a thumb, and the opening was no bigger than a toothpaste cap, so this meant that I'd have to learn how to eat all over again. Those first few sips of food were scary ones, because I didn't want to hurt my new stomach. However, the Jell-O and broth were delicious, warm, and comforting. As I savored those first few morsels, I remember thinking (probably for the first time in my life) that I finally understood how food is primarily for our survival. I took teeny, tiny bites of my cherry Jell-O, letting it melt in my mouth before I swallowed. I was beyond proud of myself because I didn't feel sick or throw up. It felt fine going down.

"As soon as you feel full, stop," my mentor, Leslie Jester, told me. Hey, what a novel concept! Why hadn't I practiced this my entire freaking life? In a nutshell, the best diet advice in the world is the following: When you feel full, put down your utensils, and that way you won't overeat. For me, that was never possible until this exact moment.

A really strange thing happened right after the operation— I couldn't wait for the moment when they allowed me out of bed to walk down the hospital hallway. It wasn't that I was so into the exercise (that would come later, shockingly), or that I was that anxious to get on my feet (although that did feel good); no, my main motivation to stand came from the desire to walk over to the scale and see proof that the entire scary experience of an operation had been worthwhile.

The first time I got on the scale, I saw that I'd *gained* 14 pounds! This was *not* in the brochure! Could I get my money

back? Or was this the worst practical joke ever played on anyone, ever?

"Carnie, don't worry," said Nurse Rosemary. "You're just
bloated with fluid from the operation, and if you wait 24 hours
and calm down, you'll get a great surprise." Rosemary was right.
The next day I lurched down the hall at a snail's pace, yet when
I got on the scale I saw that I'd lost seven of those pounds. The
following day, I was down six more. Call the newspapers!

But something awful happened during this period that I
thought was serious at first, but in retrospect was just an annoy-
ance. You always hear of the risks involved in WLS (weight-loss
surgery), and I did get a small infection (called a *seroma*) inside
one of my laproscopic incisions. Basically, it was a gross little
pocket of goo, and Leslie and my doctor had to drain it with an
orange stick, which hurt like hell. I needed shots of Novocain
because it was *that* painful. Not to freak anybody out, but the
shots went into my wound, and I needed them three times a day.
Oww! I want to be honest with people who are thinking about
the surgery, because one out of every ten people could potentially get a seroma. For all the highs involved with successful
weight loss, the infection was a small drawback for me—it was
horrible, painful, and scary, but like most things in life that can
be described in those words, it passed. And soon I was back on
the road to recovery with the help of my mom, my aunt Dee-Dee,
and Wendy. I'll never forget how they put up with my whining
and psycho outbursts of crying and joy.

After only three days, I left the hospital and moved to a hotel
close to the hospital for further recovery. I walked in that place at

266 pounds, which made me want to do a little dance, although in my condition shaking my booty was strictly out of the question. Especially when you consider that every single time my mom went over a speed bump in the hotel parking lot, I let out a big whine, and then we'd have a good laugh. We even rented a La-Z-Boy chair for me to sleep in, because that was the only way I could actually find a comfy spot for my body.

My diet at the time consisted of more water, more broth, and that fabulous Jell-O (which I grew to hate in all flavors, especially the icky lime). Ten days had passed and I had lost (drumroll, please) 22 pounds. I thought it was a miracle, and I couldn't even comprehend how this had happened to me. Then I was able to have my first solid food: three dime-sized bites from a soft-boiled egg, and three matching bites of buttered toast. Not only was it as good as a Thanksgiving dinner, but I was totally stuffed. And when I moved on up to a tiny piece of salmon (about the size of a silver dollar), I was practically orgasmic. After a few bites, I was finished, and guess what? *I wasn't hungry at all.*

How could I be full after three forkfuls of salmon? I thought about calling the people *at Ripley's Believe It or Not!,* because this was a first.

My mood was upbeat a few days later when I was sent home. Emotionally, I was in thrill mode because I was in the middle of the biggest battle of my entire life, and I was finally winning. I was totally pumped up because I didn't even care about food. That was the biggest miracle of all.

I know that a lot of what I'm relating in this chapter I already talked about in *Gut Feelings,* but I just want to fill in anybody who didn't read it. So, to reiterate old news, a few months before my surgery I met this really awesome musician named Rob Bonfiglio while I was touring with former Beach Boy Al Jardine. The only bad thing is that he lived in Philly and I was in California, but we liked each other so much that we were having a great long-distance relationship. After my surgery, I spent my nights speed-dialing Rob to tell him how strong I was being, how excited I was, and how much I missed him. He said that he couldn't wait to see me again and that he was so proud of me.

About six weeks after my surgery, Rob was out visiting me when an old flame entered the picture: spicy tuna rolls! I was craving sushi really bad because it's always been one of my favorite things to eat. I gave in, even though it was clearly too soon to eat rice. Those five little pieces of spicy tuna came back to haunt me, and quickly, too. I made Rob pull the car over somewhere on busy Beverly Glen Boulevard in Beverly Hills. It was the type of celeb sighting that you really hope won't make the gossip columns.

"Arrrgggahhhhhh! Oh God! Oh God!" I moaned in pain. "I don't know if I want to throw up, go to the john, or just sit here and die!"

Rob looked a little panic-stricken as he rubbed my face, which was contorted in agony.

What I learned later from my doctor is that the rice from the sushi expanded in my little belly beyond its capacity, and that's why I was in such pain. Imagine the feeling you get after ordering an extra-large pizza, promising to only eat a few pieces, and then discovering that you really did eat the whole thing. You're both sick and pissed, which isn't a good combo under any circumstances.

My sucky sushi situation passed (thank God), but life wasn't all sunshine and roses. Rob had to get back to work in Philly, so I was alone. Maybe I needed to fly solo because I had to devote myself full time to working on my body and changing eating habits that had taken me an entire lifetime to form. I was obediently following my four little rules: eating protein first, drinking 64 ounces of water daily, not snacking, and exercising.

Now we're not talking about putting in a TaeBo tape and becoming Kung-Fu Carnie. At the time, my exercise was baby steps from my front door to the mailbox. I also counted the trek from my bed to the garage as a major workout session, and there was an extra bonus in that journey. I kept my fantastic medical scale (the one I've had for years) out in the garage, so each morning I'd wander out there like a kid on Christmas morning, hoping to find something wonderful and unexpected under the tree.

I found something amazing on a daily basis: I lost one pound every single day during this period. When I moved the largest weight on the scale from the 250 notch to the 200 slot, I was practically hysterical. You see, in the past it hadn't mattered what diet I was on—that damn thing had always refused to budge. Each day I expected to have to slide the 250 weight back into its regular slot, but I kept moving farther and farther away from it. The whole thing was totally blowing my mind.

Unlike any other weight-loss plan I'd ever been on, I didn't let minor setbacks get me down. Sure, there was the eventual day that I wandered out to the garage and the scale didn't move from the day before. My immediate response was: "Damn, damn, damn!" But instead of telling myself that I screwed up or would never reach my goal, I just went back in the house and drank even more water than before. The water truly was the key, and I know we've all heard it about 1,000 times, but it's true: Drinking a lot of water helps you lose weight. What I didn't know is that we pee out our fat. So every single time I sat on the toilet, I imagined losing another pound. *Presto!* The next day, *two* pounds came off. For people who have been in Weight Watchers, you know that if you lose two pounds a week, it's a major cause for celebration. Two pounds in one day should mean that a national holiday is declared in your name!

Back in my bathroom, something equally celebratory was going on. I wasn't sure if it was my imagination at first, but I noticed that one of my chins was magically gone. It was like the Great Chin Fairy came in overnight and decided to do a little plastic surgery on me. I was already seeing a major change after 25 pounds, and it was incredible.

After being home for about a month and a half, Al Jardine called and asked me to join him on the road again as part of the Beach Boys Family and Friends tour. I'd really missed the band and being onstage, so I said yes and returned to the tour for a few dates.

Strangely, I wasn't worried about eating on the road. I learned how you could eat right no matter where you are, and I adopted a diet that included an egg for breakfast with a little mozzarella cheese; a teaspoon of unsweetened peanut butter for a snack (if I had to); some plain, grilled chicken breast; two bites of a vegetable or a salad; and a couple of bites of a starch (such as a potato) for lunch; and salmon, two or three bites of veggies, and a few forkfuls of a small salad with regular dressing for dinner. If I was in the mood (and I wasn't always), I'd have half a piece of bread and butter with my dinner, which was heaven on earth. This was certainly a far cry from the old days when I'd inhale an entire basket of bread—now I ate one piece and was satisfied. It's amazing how my appreciation for food had increased in such a short time.

I actually stuck to this diet (varying the protein choices) for the first six months after my surgery, and I never got sick of it. (Anyone can try it, whether they've had WLS or not. Check out the Appendix for specifics.) Meanwhile, I couldn't wait to eat a little steak. I was a little bit leery at first, since people who have had WLS often think they can't eat beef, but it went down so easily that I got really excited. The truth is that lots of people eat these big bites and then are shocked when the meat gets stuck. I say, "You wouldn't shove a big hunk of steak into a baby's mouth, would you?" It's the same thing when your stomach opening is the size of a pea. You've gotta take it *slow;* plus, your tummy is still a healing wound right after surgery.

People always ask if I was tempted to cheat the first few months after my surgery. I'd think about my boyfriend, Rob, and his hands all over my shrinking body. Believe me, it was a big deterrent when it came to cheating! I did dream about chocolate cake and different desserts, but I didn't eat them. Seeing my weight go down was the best motivation ever. In fact, it was downright unbelievable because it had previously taken me a month to lose five pounds, which I'd just put on again the next month. This time, the scale kept going down, and I was keeping the weight off. I was also completely focused on healing, because my body was still a little sore. Meanwhile, my spirits were soaring and I couldn't wait to see Rob. After I lost 30 pounds, I took a sexy picture of myself, but I never sent it to him. It was just for me—and the victory was just in *taking* the photo.

Back at Weight-Loss Central, nothing in my closet fit me anymore because I was going into a new size every two weeks. I'd wear a pair of pants, go to put them on later in the week, and they'd fall right off my ass. Yes, I was slowly waving good-bye to Miss Lane Bryant and saying, "See ya, baby." Sorry, Lane, because you did dress me well back in the day.

So I didn't become a "baggy lady." I went to Sears and JCPenney to buy some inexpensive in-between clothes. I'd find a shirt that cost $12.50, wear it a few times, and then give it to Goodwill. During this time, my closet looked a bit like a small store because I had everything from a size 28 to a size 18 in there.

And I was finally able to glare at the 28's and say with total confidence, "Never again!"

✪ ✪ ✪

chapter *Two*

Are *You* *Eating* Enough?

November 1999 to January 2000

- ✪ *Beginning weight:* 214
- ✪ *Ending weight:* 180
- ✪ *Sizes:* from 20 to 14

ight before Thanksgiving, I had dinner with my dad and my stepmom, Melinda, and something really weird happened. I was busy enjoying a little lobster, when Dad looked at me with great concern and said words I will never forget.

He didn't say, "I love you" (although he says that all the time). He didn't say, "You look great" (although he says that a lot, too). He said something even more precious to me: "Carnie, do you think you're eating enough?"

I was overjoyed on so many levels. After all, I wasn't exactly used to this phrase being thrown my way. *Are you eating enough?* Are those four of the most beautiful words in the English language or what? Of course, they pale in comparison to the times someone would say, "Wow, you're really getting skinny!" or "Don't lose *too* much weight."

Meanwhile, my doctors told me that my stomach would gradually be able to hold more and more until it could house about one cup or eight ounces of food, which is one-third to one-half the size of an average tummy. Of course, eight ounces is still quite a lot of food.

All of those years of dieting had made me sort of an amateur nutritionist, which was really helpful since I was *finally* learning how to make smart food choices. I was loving to eat what I call "clean" food, and I couldn't believe that I wasn't craving the fried stuff anymore. Sure, I'd gaze at those Duncan Hines commercials on TV and think, *Hello, lover. We've been together in the past, and we'll be together in the future, but we can no longer enjoy each other on a daily basis.*

I was doing really well in the rest of my life as well. By this time, Rob and I were madly in love with each other. I'd finally found a man who would stick by me through thick and thin. He'd fallen in love with me when I was at my heaviest, but what I weighed had nothing to do with how he felt about me. Rob has always loved me for who I am, which has nothing to do with a number on a scale. At times, I couldn't trust myself to believe that it was true, but each time I had doubts, he told me I was sexy from the start, and he proved to me again and again that he was here to stay. He loved me *completely.*

Now let's get to the good stuff. As I kept getting rid of the pounds, I became really horny. (Did someone unleash my hormones during the surgery?) All I could think about was how sexy I was feeling. I felt like buying out the entire Victoria's Secret catalog and basically driving Rob nuts. I wanted him to lose his mind when he looked at my new body, and to think about it when I wasn't with him. I was never someone who had a problem with sex and weight, but the truth is, I felt sexier and way more desirable as the weight came off. And the first time Rob and I made love during this time, I was breathless because of the way he looked at me. Later that night, he held me in a way I'll always remember. It wasn't just about the act of sex, but I felt like someone who had actually soared out of the trap of her old body into a glorious new place where I was as light as a butterfly.

I know I already told this story in *Gut Feelings,* but I love it, so here we go again. Rob came out to visit me that November, and one night we went out for a special dinner at my favorite restaurant, The Ivy. It was just one of those beautiful, easy evenings together, except I noticed that Rob seemed a tad preoccupied—he didn't seem to be that into his lobster and pasta. Anyway, I hightailed it to the ladies' room after dinner to fix my lipstick. When I came back, Rob was messing with this string hanging from his shirt. "Honey, can you help me?" he asked. "This shirt is so weird—can you pull this string off, please?"

I pulled and pulled. Man, that was one really tough string, but with my last yank, something fell in my hands: a gorgeous diamond ring. *"Oh my God!"* I cried.

"I love you, honey," he said. "Will you marry me?"

I couldn't say yes fast enough, and everyone around us clapped. It was like a scene in a movie, and it remains one of the happiest moments of my entire life.

One of the *worst* times I ever had happened a few weeks later in New York City when I agreed to go on the *Howard Stern Show*. Howard had always claimed to be a fan of mine, and since he's generally really nice to the people he likes, I thought it would be a good interview—and maybe even a little challenging, knowing Howard. I even brought along my "before" picture so I could show him how much weight I'd lost. And Rob was by my side throughout the whole thing . . . which actually turned out to be an unfortunate thing for him.

As we went on the air, Howard held up my "before" picture, and the first words out of his mouth were anything but nice. He ranted to Rob, "You were attracted to *this?* You made love to *this?* Are you crazy?"

I couldn't believe how low and mean Howard was being, but Rob carried the interview and said, "I was always attracted to Carnie and loved her for what was inside."

After the show was over, I walked downstairs in silence, barreled through the revolving door of the building, and stood outside bawling my eyes out. I continued to cry all the way to our beautiful hotel suite, and then I told Rob that I needed to take a nap to get over it. When I opened my eyes, he was standing in front of me holding two dozen roses. My honey! Now *this* was what it was all about.

As Christmas drew near, I was almost down 100 pounds. I started to wonder, *Is it cheating if you eat pumpkin pie on Christmas? Or is it really a <u>religious</u> experience in every sense of the word? Also, why didn't Santa ever mention to Mrs. Claus that she might have a little weight problem, and perhaps she should lay off going for takeout with the elves?* I guess some questions have no answers.

I went back to Philly with Rob for the holidays, and I was just so happy. We have these photos of me wearing a pretty red sweater and a big smile. It was a very mellow Christmas, and I ended up being very good about the food. I ate my protein first, had bites of dessert at the end of my meals, and didn't feel deprived of any of the holiday goodies because I tasted each one. Yet I was determined to keep losing weight—that's why I didn't stop exercising, even though it was about 20 degrees in the City of Brotherly Love. *Brrrrr!* Very early each morning before Rob went to work, I dragged my butt out of that warm comforter, kissed my man good-bye, pulled on my clunky boots, and walked outside for 45 minutes. I wasn't speed-walking by any means, I just briskly went about my business and tried not to slip on the ice. I was feeling so good because the air was crisp and invigorating, and when I thought about my promising future with Rob, that made me walk a little faster and taller.

I figured that I was definitely down about 100 pounds by now. I didn't know my exact weight because Rob didn't own a scale. When I went home in January, I discovered that I was down seven more pounds. Yes, I *had* lost 100 pounds—in other words, the unthinkable had happened. All I could do was stand in my garage and cry.

✪ ✪ ✪

chapter *Three*

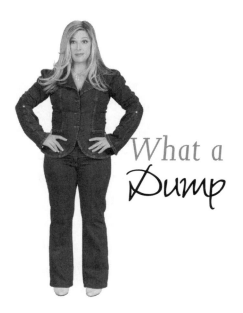

What a *Dump*

February to May 2000

- ✪ *Beginning weight:* 180
- ✪ *End weight:* 165
- ✪ *Sizes:* from 14 to 12

That winter I flew back and forth to Philly to see Rob, and I eventually moved there to be with him permanently. We now had lower long-distance bills and breakfast together, and we also shared something very precious to me (not a toothbrush—gross!). I'm talking about my medical scale, which we put in the basement next to his music workstation. There were times when I even caught Rob weighing himself!

Now that I'd lost more than 100 pounds, there were days when the scale didn't budge at all. Then the next day another pound would be history. To stay positive, I just kept remembering what my surgeon had told me: "If you do what you're told, the pounds will come off. You really should weigh yourself every day just to see how your weight fluctuates." At the same time, my friend Leslie told me to just weigh myself once a week. But I found that weighing myself daily kept me honest and on track.

As I celebrated 100 pounds off my bod, my energy level was pumped up—at least most of the time. But it was at this point that self-sabotage started to creep in. I remember walking through a mall one day, thinking, *Hmm, what if I just had a little piece of one those cinnamon pretzels? What could it hurt? Certainly I'm not going to gain 100 pounds back in one afternoon between visiting Williams-Sonoma and Macy's.* Then I did the equivalent of whacking myself upside the head, as I realized, *Stupid, self-sabotaging moments like this one are what got you in trouble in the first place!*

I've also learned that it's true what they say about a food craving—if you wait five or ten minutes, you usually won't want whatever it is anymore. Now if only sex worked that way . . . wait, we'll get to that in a later chapter. I found that if I was in that "just gotta have a taste" mood, getting a little tester size of frozen yogurt would usually do the trick. (Reminder: A "tester size" doesn't equal a scoop. It's exactly one bite.)

Anyhow, one morning before Valentine's Day, I stripped naked and stepped on the scale to learn that I'd lost 125 pounds. I was so filled with joy that I felt like I could actually fly.

That night, Rob and I didn't shoot off fireworks or call CNN, but we did celebrate this feat (as well as a new song he wrote) by having a nice candlelit dinner and listening to Frank Sinatra. It was cool, because I kept thinking, *You've lost 125 pounds, which is something you've never been able to do in the past. One hundred twenty-five pounds is the size of another person.* I called Leslie, crying. And she wept with me, because it was such a milestone.

In the next few weeks when someone would ask, "So how much weight have you lost?" I'd casually reply, "Oh, 125 pounds." It got to the point where the words flowed out of me like the chorus of a really catchy pop song. It was almost like a message should have gone over the P.A. system in the supermarket: "Attention, shoppers, Carnie Wilson, the girl in the veggie aisle, has lost 125 pounds and counting!"

Despite all my success, the unthinkable happened: Yep, I began to crave sugar again. But I was smarter now, so I usually just sucked on a Tootsie Pop after dinner each night. I can't say it enough: Try a *bite* of something you like, because most of the time you can be satisfied with just a taste. I know that there are people who have had WLS and still wander out to the fridge in the middle of the night to do some major damage. I can only imagine how sad that is for them, because they took such a bold step, only to still struggle with the old demons. And I can certainly empathize with that, because old habits are hard to break.

I kept a close watch on myself, but it wasn't always so easy. What was up with the day I made a peanut-butter pie? I honestly think that I baked that stupid dessert just to test myself. Miraculously, I only had one bite, but I had a little serving of self-doubt, too. I realized that I was trying to sabotage myself. So I stared and stared at that pie . . . and then popped a Tootsie Pop into my mouth, turned off the kitchen lights, and walked away from it. That was the only way.

What really helped was being in love. Sure, I was a little homesick, but I was happily distracted as I planned our wedding. All of the old feelings of not being good enough or worthy enough were swept away for the time being, because my mind was wrapped around starting a new life with Rob. Our life was already so beautiful, and we settled into a nice routine: I'd be doing my thing (like making us a delicious, healthy dinner) upstairs, while he created beautiful music in our basement.

Some of my optimism came crashing down one night when we had a small dinner party for some friends. For dessert, I'd made Jell-O with pieces of real fruit and topped with Cool Whip Lite. Okay, it's not exactly something that *Bon Appétit* would push, but it seemed light, easy, and relatively healthy to me because I made sure to use the sugar-free Jell-O that I'd eaten in the hospital. (Yes, I could suddenly stand it again). Well, that marked my first experience with "dumping" (when too much sugar is "dumped" into your small intestine), which is common in WLS patients.

You see, I never realized just how much sugar is in Cool Whip Lite. (This is the very reason why a lot of people continue to gain weight even though they eat all those so-called light foods.) When something's lower in fat, it's always higher in sugar; if it doesn't have sugar, you get the fat back. Sorry to ruin your day with this news. Anyway, let me just tell you that dumping is the most horrible feeling in the world. Your heart beats really fast, you're sweating, your nose gets totally stuffy, and you feel really dizzy. It's like a panic attack combined with a terrible stomachache *and* a horrible cold. Basically, there isn't a part of your body that's doesn't feel like total shit. Hitting your bed is about the only option you have (short of calling your doctor), so that's what I did.

"I'm sorry, everybody. I have to go upstairs and lie down for a little bit," I told our guests, trying to hide some of my panic as I ran up the stairs.

Rob followed me because he was really worried. He spent the next few minutes just rubbing my head and my hands and saying, "Just calm down. It's going to be okay."

"But we have company downstairs," I argued.

"Who cares?" he said. "Just lie here until it goes away." And that's exactly what we did. He cuddled up with me until I was finished dumping. What an angel—my dumping angel!

I had other world-class dumping experiences, too. On a visit back to Los Angeles, I ate some Carbolite yogurt with a few carob chips, and the honey in the chips made me so ill that I wanted to die. I thought I'd have to be taken to the emergency room, but my friend Katrina was with me at the time and she just rubbed my feet, brought me a cold washcloth for my forehead, and helped me pray that it would pass. I learned my lesson that day, and I know now that if something is really sweet or high in fat, I can only have a couple of bites. As if to drive that point home, one night Rob and I went to a club to see some jazz musicians. I had four bites of cheesecake as a sort of experiment, and I didn't feel too good. I didn't exactly dump, but I felt very tired, which is a warning sign. (And those were little bites!)

Speaking of things biting, showbiz actually bit me in the behind during this period of my life. The shows with Al dried up because of unfortunate lawsuits concerning who could call themselves The Beach Boys. In the past, that sort of work upset would have sent me straight to a box of See's Candies, but that was simply not an option. Now I had to figure out ways to cope that didn't include overeating. I found that I'd feel better by taking an extra-long walk, calling a friend, or (of course) talking things over with Rob. I'm not saying that I didn't give in and eat a few more nuts than I should have or scarf down an extra piece of cheese when I got off the phone after hearing shitty work news, but I tried to stop myself with a firm, "No. Stop." Sometimes I'd spit stuff into the trash and say, "You don't really want that. This is an old habit. Break it!"

I couldn't believe I had this willpower. I actually began a daily ritual of thanking God for my new body *and* my new mind-set.

At this time, I was continuing to do my work with **SpotlightHealth.com,** a company that supported me 100 percent through my surgery and had me post updates and record my progress on-line to help other people. Certain people criticized me for revealing so much about my personal life, but you know what? These critics and cynics weren't next to me on

Rob's computer that winter and spring when someone truly in need of help would instant-message me with a story that made my mascara run.

For instance, one day I was online with Brenda and Kristy, a mother and daughter who wrote me to say that they'd had WLS together; in fact, they'd gone under the knife on the same day. Can you even imagine the stress on that family? Together, they weighed almost 700 pounds—Brenda was 360 pounds; and Kristy, her daughter, was 330 pounds. Think about their health concerns, their physical pain, their shame, and so forth for a minute. I didn't have to imagine it because I'd lived it. And somehow my being so up-front made other people, such as Brenda and Kristy, feel like they'd lived it with me.

I decided to invite them to a concert I was doing in their hometown of Fresno, California. Brenda and Kristy were two years post-op at the time and had lost more than half of their body weight. When we finally met in person, it was like we were three survivors hugging each other for dear life. There we were at the back of the tour bus, comparing body parts and discussing how our skin was rapidly changing. Brenda and Kristy were both bundles of energy and had great attitudes. They were my first real connection with people who'd had WLS, and they really inspired me.

I figured that as the pounds fell off, loose skin was also going to be an issue for me. Pretty soon, I was noticing this useless skin flapping over on my stomach and arms, and it made me extremely sad. I'd touch the loose skin and watch it dance around while wondering, *Will I ever have the body I want? Will I <u>ever</u> be satisfied, or will my fat somehow always haunt me for the rest of my life?*

✪ ✪ ✪

chapter *Four*

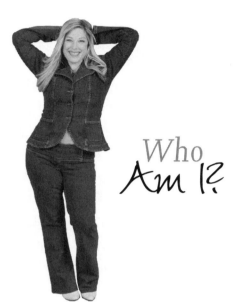

Who Am I?

June to August 2000

- ✪ *Beginning weight:* 165
- ✪ *End weight:* 155
- ✪ *Sizes:* from 12 to 10

Good-bye fat, hello fame. When I'd lost almost 150 pounds, the media decided that there might be something to this new, thinner Carnie that could sell magazines and get ratings. So I plastered on my best Cover Girl smile and got back out there. Of course the press also thought that I was in love with my bod and spent every single moment in some state of euphoria, or at the very least, naked in front of the bathroom mirror. I hated to burst anyone's bubble, but I still despised my thighs. Sometimes I made jokes at their expense ("Wow, it's a miracle that there's actually a space between them!").

Soon I'd appeared on *The View, Entertainment Tonight, Extra, Leeza,* and CNN. I decided to give Howard Stern another shot, and this time he was really, really nice to me. I told him how I was down 150 pounds, and he said, "Well, you know, Carn, you still need to lose 40 more. But you look great." During the commercial break, he grabbed me, hugged me, and said, "I'm so proud of you. You look fabulous. I'd do you." *Hello!*

People, Us Weekly, and *Woman's World* magazines put me on their covers, and I gave them all a huge smile, since more than ten million people were about to see that I had a waistline. Yes, my hips were now up for public consumption, and the letters that poured in were both pleasing and upsetting. Some people wrote that I'd taken the easy way out by being a rich girl who could afford WLS. I wanted to scream that I'd been on a serious weight-loss plan for many months now, pushing desserts aside, taking all those vitamins, drinking 64 ounces of water every single day, exercising five days a week . . . hey, that was anything but easy. It was continual hard work. This wasn't about just being good for a week and then giving in and blowing a diet like I'd done a million times before. I took great pride in what I'd accomplished. Oh, and for you people who said that I could afford the surgery because I was rich, well, my health insurance covered the operation. And did you know that at that time I was about to declare bankruptcy?

Oprah even invited me on her show. This was quite a milestone, because she's not a big fan of WLS. However, she listened and was respectful, and I thought it was brave of her to have me on because this certainly was a hot-button issue for her, too.

Sure, you may have seen me smiling all over the place, but inside I wasn't always so happy, even though all those pounds were now gone. In my mind, I'd always blamed my fat as the one thing in my life that was a roadblock to total joy. Lose the lard—instant happiness! Unfortunately, it didn't exactly work that way. Now I don't think that I really anticipated a life where I was tiptoeing through the tulips every single second once I lost half of myself. But now that I was closer to my goal, my new mind-set was starting to worry me.

The media had dubbed me "The new Carnie Wilson." Excuse me, but what happened to the *old* Carnie Wilson? I began to ask myself one question: *Who the hell is that new girl?*

At night I'd stare into the dark, and Rob would notice that I was still awake.

"What's wrong?" he'd ask.

"I don't know," I'd whisper. "I just don't feel right. I'm really glad that I lost all this weight, but I'm also scared. I feel like I want to cry because I'm not sure who I am anymore—and what am I going to do when I lose *all* the weight? What will my life be about then? What will be left?"

Rob would respond, "Baby, you've just got to get used to your new body and your new self. I promise it will get easier. I'm here with you. I'm not going anywhere."

Since I struggled with abandonment issues, this struck a deep chord with me. I couldn't get over how patient and gentle Rob was. He really helped me get through things . . . but when he wasn't around, stuff tended to get a bit tricky.

I remember the day someone insisted that I wasn't me. I was walking around the streets of New York on a business trip trying to chill out before I gave a speech about gastric-bypass surgery to a room filled with people who needed some serious inspiration (plus a few doctor types, too). A handsome young man approached me, and since he didn't look like he had a prison record, I stopped and smiled when we made eye contact.

"You look so familiar to me, but I just can't place who you are," he said in the sweetest voice.

"This happens to me all the time," I replied, feeling proud because all the press I'd done had really gotten the word out about morbid obesity, and it was nice to know that my face was recognizable even though it wasn't exactly the round ball it used to be.

I waited a minute for this guy to place me, but as a couple of hours seemed to pass and he was no closer to deciding if I was Carnie Wilson or Jackie Wilson, I decided to put the poor sap out of his misery.

"I'm Carnie Wilson," I said.

"No, you're not," he said, but his words didn't carry an exclamation point, as in, "No way, sister!" They were almost accusatory, like, "No, you're absolutely not her, so quit lying about it!"

"Really, I *am* Carnie," I repeated, stating it with a little shock.

At this point, the guy looked me right in the eye and demanded, "Carnie Wilson? The singer? The one on TV?"

I nodded patiently, because he apparently didn't get a good look at me the first time and probably wasn't expecting to see actual cheekbones on my face. I smiled and waited for the inevitable apology or embarrassed look when the guy realized how he'd been so wrong.

Instead, he gave me a much slower once-over, closed his eyes, and shook his head. "No, you're *definitely* not her," he concluded.

Suddenly, I had an idea. "Would you like to see my driver's license so I can prove it to you?" I asked sweetly.

"Yes, I would," he said with attitude. In shock, he grabbed it and said, "I can't believe it. You look so different."

"As you can see, it's me, Carnie. Nice to meet you," I said.

"Is that a fake ID?" the guy asked with narrow eyes.

After WLS, I had an entirely new identity, although there was nothing fake about it. I was still a real person . . . wasn't I?

Marc, my therapist, explained that it was almost like I'd experienced the death of my former self, and I was in the process of grieving for her. But I knew it was also something else. I was transforming into someone new, and I didn't even know how to feel about myself anymore. Which me were we even talking about—the old me or the new me?

This whole identity crisis hit me hard when Spotlight Health asked me to go on various lecture tours to talk about my weight loss as a way to help professionals in the field and people who really needed to save their lives. So there I was one day standing at this podium in Philly looking at all these serious pharmaceutical reps who didn't seem to have any expressions on their faces. I was strangely nervous when I walked out onstage and faced these guys, but I didn't have time to dwell on the butterflies in my now-smaller stomach. Soon, Richard Hull, the president and CEO of Spotlight Health, introduced me: "And now, one of our most wonderful success stories . . . Carnie Wilson!"

I knew the drill, which began with watching a video of me before the surgery. My parents and Wendy were on the tape, and just watching them made me feel so emotional, even if it was the umpteenth time I'd seen it. Mom was up there crying, and Wendy looked in the camera and said, "I wanted my sister to do the surgery so she could live longer." The most difficult part of the tape was when Dad popped up on-screen, sitting at the piano and singing, "Don't worry, Carnie, everything will turn out all right." It was my personal version of The Beach Boys' hit song, "Don't Worry, Baby." Talk about heart-wrenching—watching it almost made me lose my composure.

That day, it hit me that the 300-pound girl up on that screen was someone I knew about 100 years ago, but I just couldn't relate to her anymore. I couldn't even understand her. Some people would say that this illustrated how far I've come, but that wasn't it. In my heart, even though that girl seemed so far away from me, she still was a part of me. I felt scared for her. I realized that nobody could really even see my face through all that fat. I couldn't even remember being that big.

I didn't have time to dwell on these feelings because the spotlight was suddenly on me. My thinner self felt strange walking out onto that stage because for the first time ever, I felt very vulnerable. All that fat was gone, and for a split second I thought, *I'm no match for these people.* Then I shook it off, grabbed the microphone, and said, "Hello, I'm Carnie Wilson." This seemed to convince everyone including myself. Yes, I am and always will be Carnie Wilson, damn it!

Later, I wondered, *Is there a bigger problem? Am I afraid of change?* I was so used to disappointments when it came to weight loss that I was actually numb when each diet didn't work. I had no fear of failure . . . because I never really thought I'd succeed. But with WLS, I knew that this time I really was going to make it. (That's the attitude I encourage people to have.)

Perhaps I was actually developing a fear of success, which is almost harder to deal with. It's like that old adage, "Be careful what you wish for because you just might get it." And I'd add: "You might get your wish and then be in even deeper shit."

If we succeed, we're often afraid that we'll lose what we achieved, or we worry that we're not worthy of it. That's why many of us succeed at something and then purposely sabotage it—we just don't feel as if we deserve it. We don't always excel at feeling good and being at peace because we're not exactly conditioned to know how to feel strong, successful, and worthy. *Total* bliss? Please. Most of us wouldn't know it if it hit us over the head.

After 30 years of wanting this thinner body, I was practically there. I wondered what would happen when I did reach the promised land of size six (or whatever the ultimate in weight loss would be for me). Would I stand there and weep for joy? Or would I look at that new, narrower face in the mirror and say: "Now what?" Knowing myself, the smart money was on choice B.

My fears were put to rest (at least temporarily) on June 23, 2000, when I married Rob at the Hotel Bel-Air in Los Angeles. It thrilled me to the core that my father walked me down the aisle and Wendy was my maid of honor. As for the dress—well, I'd found one that slid off my shoulders, poufed out on the bottom, and had a huge train made of beautiful, antique lace. It pissed me off that it was a size 16, but the wedding-dress ladies assured me that in real sizes it would be more like a size 12. I don't really understand this thinking—I mean, why don't they make them to reflect a smaller size? If someone had said, "Miss Wilson, we're sorry, but our dresses run so large that you'll have to get married in a size eight, if that's okay with you!" well, that really would have been the happiest day of my life!

No matter, it really *was* my happiest day. After all, I was getting married to my soul mate, and 130 pounds were gone from my frame. In fact, a couple of days before the wedding, the dress I'd originally chosen was suddenly too big. It was so much work to alter that I decided to get another dress—a simple, inexpensive, white matte-satin dress with lace sleeves and a scoop neck. I didn't want the poufing-out part anymore either (I had poufed out for enough years, thank you very much). My hair was styled in a Spanish bun with gardenias strewn in it. I looked simple and elegant.

For someone who had spent a lifetime performing, I was surprisingly nervous as I walked down the aisle through the hotel's lush garden. I would have married Rob anywhere, but I was so happy to be able to hold my father's arm and gaze at the 220 people who had come to share this day with us. Even my WLS surgeon, Dr. Alan Wittgrove, flew in on the red-eye for the ceremony.

When Rob gazed at me at the altar with tears in his eyes, I lost it completely and didn't give a damn about my makeup. Everyone around us was crying, too, and this continued right through the father-daughter dance.

I chose "Be My Baby" by the Ronettes, which is my father's favorite song. He told me it was perfect. Of course, that made me cry even harder, and Dad held me and said, "Aw, I love you, Carnie. Please don't cry." I wasn't sad; these were tears of happiness because, after all those years, my father and I were exactly where we belonged—dancing together in each other's arms.

★

After our big day, Rob and I went back to Philadelphia. I still felt a little homesick there, but that didn't stop me from losing weight. Al Jardine continued to be tied up in lawsuits, so I wasn't working regularly. This really left me feeling nervous because I'm the type of person who always needs to be moving forward. Somehow I found the wisdom to just put on the brakes and enjoy my first few months as a married woman.

Rob and I went on our beautiful honeymoon in Italy—we spent 16 days celebrating the joy and awe of the most fabulous, glorious country in the world. The only downer was that the plane ride there made me so constipated (something common for WLS patients who don't drink all their water) that I swear there was a brick at the bottom of my ass. I had to place an emergency phone call to Leslie to ask her for some advice. "What the heck do I do?" I begged. She told me to get some milk of magnesia. Believe me, it was a real gas (ha-ha!) trying to find milk of magnesia in an Italian pharmacy. There I was, saying, "Milko? Magnesio? Need to poop-o?"

Yes, I ate a little bread and pasta in Italy—who would miss that part of the trip? I really watched the portions, and my new hubby and I made up for it by walking all over the place. I lost six pounds, while Rob gained eight! For the first time, *I* told *him,* "Honey, you don't look like you've gained a pound to me."

He worked it off once we got back to Philly because Rob became my exercise partner, which was a nice way for us to spend part of the day. It's not like we were climbing mountains, but the exercise, combined with my diet, meant that the scale was now registering 155 pounds.

✪ ✪ ✪

chapter Five

It's
Still Me

September to December 2000

- ✪ *Beginning weight:* 153
- ✪ *End weight:* 148
- ✪ *Sizes:* from 8 to 6

One freaky thing about losing half of what I used to weigh is that nobody knew how to react to the new me. All everybody seemed to focus on was the change in my body; meanwhile, I wondered if they could see the same heart and the same mind that had always been there.

When all of this got to be too much for me, Rob would put it all in perspective. He'd gently take my hand and say, "Honey, be still with things. Just be in the moment right now. Know you're safe. You're here. I'm here. Be still."

Did I mention that my husband is just about the smartest man on the planet?

Oh, by the way, it was a little intense when someone would see me and then shout from across the gym/store/restaurant/restroom stall: "*Oh my God!* I never would have recognized you! You look so good!" Notice that I said "intense," not "bad." Who am I kidding? Those words felt damn good. But what sort of threw me is when people started screaming (something about weight loss makes people want to yell): "*You are a totally different person!*" I understood where these people were coming from, but it really messed with my head. It was like they were saying, "You're not yourself. You're not you anymore."

And sometimes my own shit got thrown back in my face. My friend Robin's mother, a wonderful woman named Marty, had WLS the year before and lost 140 pounds. (Robin, who also had the surgery and lost more than 140 pounds, inspired her mom—and eventually her dad, too, who's lost 85 pounds in three months.) Well, one day we all went out for sushi before going to a support-group meeting. Yes, I'd found a local group in my area that supported WLS patients, and it was an invaluable resource, because we were all changing rapidly and found comfort and support sharing everything together. We've been a group for more than two years now.

Anyway, I hadn't seen Marty for a while, and I was really stunned. She looked amazing, like she was 30 years old again

In a louder-than-normal voice, I exclaimed, "Oh my God, Marty, you look like a totally different person!"

I could see her looking a little bit uncomfortable, and I instantly felt really bad. And this thought raced through my mind: *Now I know what it's like on the other side.*

So I tried again: "What I meant to say is, 'Oh my God, you look incredibly beautiful, Marty.'"

This time, she melted into the most joyous smile, hugged me, and whispered, "You look so incredibly beautiful, too, Carn. If it wasn't for you, none of this would have happened for me."

I was overjoyed, but also taken aback, as I realized that I was now a role model for weight loss, of all things. Mind-boggling!

Meanwhile, I was coping with this identity-crisis, fear-of-success bullshit, and it was definitely time to get some help. First, I turned to Leslie. Since she'd also had WLS and had lost half of *her* former self, she could set me straight.

"To begin with, you're still you where it counts the most," she told me. "You just have to figure out a new way to deal with the outside you, and that's going to take some time. After all, it didn't take you six months to become 300 pounds. It will also take some time to learn to live in your new body. The first step is to be proud of what you worked so hard for."

Now what about my fear of success? This is where Marc, my therapist, came in. "Carnie, it's called the 'let-down effect,'" he explained. "When people suffer from something and then they find relief, they often become depressed. When they've done something great and it's over, they can also become depressed or even physically ill."

"I think I'm becoming a little depressed," I admitted.

"That's totally normal. You see, we use a lot of anxiety and energy to reach a goal," he said. "When the goal is reached, it's easy to transfer those emotions and turn them into depression. There's almost a sadness when we attain what we want because the getting-there part is over."

I guess it's that morning-after-Christmas feeling. I also remember feeling that sadness when we'd finish a long Wilson Phillips tour. Anyway, I started thinking those two annoying words again: *Now what?*

During interviews, I talked about how lucky I was to have my new body, but something else was happening inside me. I was becoming even more nervous when it came to the emotions I was now experiencing. See, I knew how to be the fat girl whose pain was underneath all of that padding—but as a thinner woman, I suddenly felt as if someone had exposed me to the whole world.

"I don't even feel like myself anymore!" I cried to Leslie. "That scares me deep inside. I mean, who am I now?"

She reminded me that the fat I'd protected myself with all those years didn't just come about from a love for food, but stemmed from something much deeper—my fear of being out there for everyone to see.

"Now it seems like each pound I lose gets me more to the core of who I am. Do I even know that person?" I asked her.

One day it dawned on me that I still had most of the same problems I had before my surgery. I still had a childhood that wasn't perfect. I still had body-image issues. I could still be sad, stressed, anxious, jealous, you name it. I just couldn't use "two all-beef patties, special sauce, lettuce, cheese" as a cure anymore. I didn't need a therapist to tell me that food was no longer the answer.

And that's when Leslie said, "You need to turn inward and really look at your life."

Shit. Look at my life? That was scarier than going through surgery.

Much to my displeasure, I discovered that the moments of sadness I had when I was fat were now the same moments of sadness in a thinner person.

Whoa—where was the "disappointment chapter" in the weight-loss manual? Yet it was at this point that I finally realized that I couldn't dwell on the past forever.

★

The past took a backseat as I dealt with the present, including the decision Rob and I made to move to Los Angeles. It was up to me to fly back and forth between the two places to find us a house, and again, being on an airplane wasn't always so good for my health. I kept experiencing that fabulous airborne combo of being dehydrated and constipated. (Don't even get me started about the hygiene of trying to go to the bathroom in those little airplane johns where the guy before you not only peed on the seat, but also on the walls, the floor, and the sink.)

Finally, Rob and I settled in Los Angeles, and I was thrilled to be back around my mom, sister, and really close friends. We were still newlyweds, so everything was fresh and exciting, from the chicken dishes I served up to the new lingerie I bought. I'd put one of those little strappy outfits on and think, *Wow—a year ago, this strap would have had to be made out of the toughest leather to hold things up.*

This was a happy, sexy, thrilling time. Rob and I shared many fun-filled days and nights together—we'd go in-line skating or take long walks, and we adored going out for dinner. I'd laugh when he'd look at my plate of chicken and mashed potatoes and ask me tenderly, "Are you sure you can have that?"

"Honey, I've lost more than 150 pounds," I'd calmly reassure him. "I think I *know* if I can have something."

Later we'd order dessert, and I knew that I'd only be able to have one bite of the apple tart . . . okay, maybe two. Yet when the waiter left the bubbling, hot, gooey thing in front of us, and I'd go for my fork, Rob would joke, "Honey, be careful. You're going to dump."

Sometimes he was right, sometimes he was wrong. I knew what my limits were, but there were a couple of nights when I called his name from the bedroom after we got home from dinner. I'd moan, "Honey, I'm dumping!"

He'd respond, "You see, I told you, baby." (Two points for my dumping angel.)

✪ ✪ ✪

chapter Six

Falling into the Skinny Gap

January to April 2001

- ✪ *Beginning weight:* 148
  (the beginning of maintenance)
- ✪ *End weight:* fluctuating from 147 to 152
- ✪ *Sizes:* from 8 to 6

After the holidays, I was hitting the sales for Rob (yeah, right) when I walked into a Gap to try on some boot-cut stretch blue jeans.

After losing all the weight, I wasn't really sure what size I was now in jeans. So I grabbed a pair of size-10s and mentally prepared myself for the usual Olympian event of tugging on a new pair of jeans. I was just hoping that I didn't break a nail or start sweating above my upper lip like I would in the old days. But a funny thing happened on the way to size 10. I put on the jeans and noticed that I wasn't sucking in my gut at all. The zipper wasn't even my enemy—in fact, I actually liked the sound as it easily slid on up to the top. I couldn't believe it . . . they were loose.

There isn't a lot of room in those Gap dressing rooms to do what I call "the happy dance." No matter—I turned that dressing room into the stage at Carnegie Hall, and I danced my little heart out.

"Can I help you?" asked the helpful Gap girl, and I couldn't believe that these words came out of my mouth: "These are a little bit big on me. Could I please try a size 8?" Yet when she brought those babies in, they were also a little roomy. She was catching on to what was happening and practically started dancing with me!

When I bought my first pair of size-6 jeans, I did the happy dance all the way back to the car. I also wanted to cut the tag out of the jeans, enlarge it, and frame it. Of course, I never did that, because Rob might have thought that I'd finally gone nuts.

Size six! *Six freaking six!* The reality hit me as I said the following words to myself: *"I am actually petite."*

Whoa! What a concept!

✪ ✪ ✪

chapter *Seven*

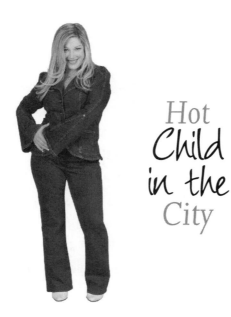

Hot
Child
in the
City

May to September 2001

- ✪ *Weight:* Maintaining for more than a year
- ✪ *Sizes:* from 8 to 6

That summer I received an e-mail with a photo of a very happy, glowing woman. The message said: "Here's a picture of you and me from an appearance you did. I've lost 179 pounds because of you. I just want you to know that I was paralyzed and in a wheelchair for six and a half years because of my weight, which was about 320 pounds when I stopped counting. I took Fen-Phen and had a stroke. I didn't care about the medical problems back then—I kept taking the drug because I would have done *anything* to lose weight. And then I read your story. I immediately looked into WLS and found the courage to do it. . . . I know you'll probably never see this e-mail, but I just wanted you to know that I owe you my life. I also wanted you to know that I put my wheelchair to rest on April 10. Forever. I have two new knees, and a new diamond ring that my husband just bought me. People no longer call me 'Wheeling Around.' My new nickname is 'Walking Tall.' Carnie, I love you and admire you. I'm 57 years old and have a new life. Thank you and God bless."

When people knock me for having this surgery, I want to take this letter, which I cherish, and wave it around like a flag. And it makes *me* walk a little bit taller, too. This is just the tip of the iceberg when it comes to the letters I receive. I read every single one of them, and I'm extremely touched and happy for everyone.

✪

After keeping the weight off for almost two years, it was time for me to touch base with my career. I was thinking of the various options I had when I was reminded of one of my favorite "comeback" stories.

Rob and I had flown to Las Vegas to attend the Billboard Music Awards, which is a major annual music event. I was going to be a presenter, and it was the first time I'd "unveiled" the new me in such a live, public way. So I needed to make sure I looked like hot shit. To that end, my cousin's girlfriend, Rona, made me this fabulous pantsuit out of the softest chocolate-brown suede and sequins. The top had a low, sexy neckline, and I wore these really cool faux-crocodile boots. My hair was very long (thank you, hair extensions!) and hot-mama reddish brown, and my eyeshadow was turquoise and sparkling (thank you, Kim).

Going through the line of a hundred flashing photographers was an out-of-body experience because this was the first time many of them had seen me since I'd lost the weight. I actually heard some of these usually nasty photographers gasp when they saw me—this should have made me proud, but it actually embarrassed me. For an instant, I flashed back to the award shows Wilson Phillips had gone to, and I knew that Wendy and Chynna had always felt the way I was feeling right now. Back then, I was so heavy yet trying to feel sexy for even a second in my huge custom-made pants and big blazer that hid everything. All I can say is that it felt much better to arrive feeling good about my body instead of projecting this ashamed "don't-look-at-me" vibe.

We went inside, and I got ready to present.

"Please welcome back Carnie Wilson," said a sexy-voiced announcer.

When I walked out onstage that night, the audience of 30,000 went silent for a moment, as if they thought it might be an imposter. When people realized that it looked an awful lot like one-half of the former me, they quickly jumped to their feet to give me a standing ovation. I was absolutely overwhelmed.

"Thank you, thank you," I said into the mike, as I glanced around me. Did I mention that I was surrounded by testosterone in the form of the adorable boy band 98 Degrees? I won't mention which of those Degrees was checking out my new ass, but it did happen. At that point, I just couldn't resist adding a little humor to the event. The producers *had* told me to improvise, so I was just following orders.

"I don't know what happened, but ever since I lost all the weight, I've been feeling very horny," I said, and the crowd erupted with applause.

"Being up here with these guys is great. Maybe I'd like to feel a little slap on my butt from them," I teased.

Well, I didn't have to ask twice, because the hands that millions of teenage girls dream about were suddenly on my butt. (If I'd been 12 years old again, I would have written in my diary: *I will never wash these cheeks again.*)

It might have been a lot of fun, but I wonder if anyone noticed that that night was the first time in the history of the music industry that anyone was ever celebrated at an awards show for being a loser. And you know what? It felt fantastic.

✪ ✪ ✪

Part II

The Big Head Trip
(Who Knew?)

• Introduction to Part II

I really didn't want to begin this section by talking about my mother being naked, but this part of the book is about stripping away certain emotional and physical barriers. Now what does this have to do with *my mom* being nude? Well, believe it or not, she actually wouldn't mind my telling you this because it's the cleanest of all possible stories. A first for me!

One of my favorite memories of being a little girl is sitting on the cold tile floor in Mom's bathroom while she took a bath. I just loved how the room was filled with steamy air that smelled like Rive Gauche perfume, Rachel Perry foot cream, and whatever shampoo Farrah Fawcett was hawking that particular year. Most of my ten-year-old-girl problems would begin to be solved the minute the bathwater began to run. I'd pour it all out to Mom— "Why am I always the fattest kid in my class?" "I don't want to go to Weight Watchers camp again"—while she sloshed around.

By the time she pulled the stopper out of the soapy water, many of my problems would seemingly go down the drain as well. I also loved to watch my mother get out of the tub because from my position on the floor, I could see her shake each foot off until all that hit the ground were ten perfectly manicured toes. At that point, I didn't care what was wrong with the world—those toes were heaven to me, and I wanted to be just like my mom.

I realize that confessing I sat there watching while my naked mother take a bath might be considered a topic for *Jenny Jones,* but I still long for those nightly therapy sessions. I knew I wasn't alone and that Mom could figure it all out. I guess the real bummer is that I have to explore the misty areas of my mind alone these days—without the smell of any Wella products.

As I deal with my feelings these days, I can carefully fill my own emotional tub, or I can let things overflow. I can also dunk my head underwater where it's very murky. . . .

Today I'm faced with a new phase in my life and new things to experience. That's also what this part of the book covers. It's about how I've surfaced and learned not to stuff my feelings down with food or drugs—I've actually discovered how to relieve stress and get high naturally. I had to do this by working on both the inside and the outside—*ugh*.

We'll start with the physical and then move on to the emotional. Let me tell you, dealing with the fat on my ass was way easier than dealing with the fat between my ears. The head trip was about to begin, and I had an E-ticket—to where, I didn't know. Now that the seat belt was actually fitting, I buckled it really tight, because I had a feeling it was going to be a bumpy ride.

✪ ✪ ✪

chapter Eight

Shedding Excess Skin
(Eww! Gotta Talk about It)

It was almost like a weird fairy tale: Once upon a time, a girl lost 150 pounds and lived happily ever after . . . except when she was in her wonderful bathtub, a favorite hangout spot that she inherited from her loving mother. During those times, her new, thin bod would be soaking up bubbles, and then something horrific would happen—all of her old loose skin would float to the top of the tub and even emerge through the suds.

Yep, that's what happened to me. I'd sit in the bath and play with my folds of skin, which felt like the weirdest form of human Jell-O. It was really strange, because by 2001 I was working out seriously (more on that later), and I could see and feel my muscles and bones—yet in certain areas of my body, they were hidden under a tent of useless skin. It was such a humbling, defeating, oh-shit step backwards, even though I'd lost the weight and was pushing myself at the gym. I was trying to make my body the best it could be, yet I'd look down at my stomach and see all this skin hanging down from it. I just felt like it wasn't a part of my body anymore. That's when I knew it had to go.

Like countless other species in the wild, I needed to shed my skin.

It's too bad I wasn't a snake—why couldn't I just crawl off into the desert, shed, and be done with it? Unfortunately, that wasn't possible, so I did the next best thing on the evolutionary scale: I called a plastic surgeon.

Of course, the minute I even began to think about it, it was as if the tabloids were reading my mind. I began to read that I was having "super-secret plastic surgery," which they reported like it was some sort of national crime (those prying jerk-offs).

For a long time now, I haven't cared what those scumbag papers wanted to print. I knew deep down, as my family, friends, and husband did, that I'd worked as hard as I possibly could to get the best body for me. And now I needed a little assist. So, about one million talks and two million brochures later, I faced the facts of going under the knife. I knew I'd be taking a risk when it came to the outcome, so I didn't expect perfection, just an improvement.

Since it always helps to have a surgeon with tons of experience, I chose Dr. Steven Zax in Beverly Hills. More than anything, I wanted to lift my breasts because they looked like two sports socks with nipples hanging at the bottom of them. I'm not kidding. I was a D-cup when I was heavy, and now I was a small and saggy B. I was really ashamed of my boobs, so most of all, I was looking forward to this part of the deal.

However, my tummy tuck was one of the most emotional things I've done since having WLS. On the one hand, I knew that I could do five million sit-ups and the skin would still be there; on the other hand, I could have the surgery and my stomach could possibly be flat as a board (if, of course, I continued to eat the right way and exercise). But I was used to wrapping my hands around my middle like a security blanket. It was a habit I formed many years ago. For whatever reason (probably insecurity), I learned to just grab it when I was reacting to something funny, sad, or anything in between. Letting it go was a traumatic thing for me to decide to do. What would I rest my hands on now?

I wasn't so much afraid of the pain as I was the idea that the very last trace of the familiar—my once-full skin—would be gone forever, but I'd have a flat stomach for the first time in my life. I'm not going to lie—this decision was a combination of health and vanity. I finally decided that I wanted that outer shell cut off and gone forever. *Hasta la vista,* loose skin. You won't be back.

Now the stats: Some 50 percent of gastric-bypass patients, or people who lose a tremendous amount of weight, decide to have their loose skin removed. It really is an individual decision—sometimes it's medically necessary; sometimes you just can't stand looking at the hanging skin anymore. If it really gets to you (like it did me), then have it removed. And fight with your insurance company, because some of these procedures are covered.

I was told that I should be within 10 to 15 pounds of my goal weight for best results (I was 10 pounds away). It was also important to exercise and get the muscles forming underneath the skin so that I'd have a smaller scar. I was pretty excited and got myself in good shape before I had my reconstructive surgery. I'd dream about tight jeans and those little midriff tops, but as time passed, I just wanted to get it over with. It couldn't happen soon enough!

A lot of people ask me about the pain involved in having plastic surgery, and I can't lie. It wasn't that painful, but the tummy tuck did produce the tightest pulling sensation I've ever felt in my life. It was like someone took all my fat there and squeezed it as hard and as much as possible. (I know you're probably trying this right now, so please don't hurt yourself!)

I can also tell you that post-op, I had to pay close attention to my wounds and bandages, as well as what positions I slept in. I couldn't raise my arms above my head for a few weeks, and I really had to move slowly for many weeks longer than I expected. In fact, I had to keep a close watch on my every move so I didn't hurt my incision areas. Oh, but it was so worth it!

As for the particulars, I did my surgery in Dr. Zax's office, and then recovered for three days at a private retreat in Los Angeles. This was one of those places where people disappear for a few days to have their "work" done, although they usually pretend that they're either on vacation or helping out at their local homeless shelter. It's a lot like taking your car to a really swanky mechanic. *Presto!* Your front end is suddenly damage free from a lifetime of abuse, and your rear bumper . . . well, those dents are easily put in or taken out, depending on your preference.

I actually wished that I'd gone home to recover with a nurse or even with my mom. As I sat in that luxurious room at the retreat, I longed to just be home with Rob and the dogs. Three days later, I did go home, and then the real healing began.

My boobs were especially fun. I mean, there's nothing like waking up from surgery and seeing stitches plus really icky yellow-and-purple bruises there, too. If I would have heard that Rod Stewart song "Do Ya Think I'm Sexy?" I would have burst into tears. I felt like Frankenstein and Cher at the same time. Thankfully my breasts and tummy were changing and healing a little bit every day, but they were so sore for about a month.

I just had to allow my new body to heal at its own pace, but I did heal very quickly. Part of the reason for this was because Dr. Zax made me go to a hyperbaric chamber, where I lay in a clear cylinder and breathed 100-percent oxygen for an hour at a time. It was pretty costly, but it really worked. People who have diabetes or wounds that won't heal should check this treatment out—it can be miraculous.

What also helped me was that I mentally approached my plastic surgery the same way I took on my gastric bypass. To heal, I listened to hypnosis tapes, drank a lot of water, and followed my doctor's instructions carefully—for example, Dr. Zax is obsessed with taking tons of vitamins before and even months after this surgery, so I did this religiously.

If you get grossed out easily, don't read this next section, but it's hilarious—no ifs, ands, or butts about it. Okay, when I had my first consultation with Dr. Zax, he told me that while he was doing all this work, he could also repair an old hernia I had on my lower abdomen.

Smiling, I replied, "Do me a favor and pull my lower stomach up as high as you can so my everything else (wink, wink) gets a little lift, too." So he did.

The first time I went "number two" after the operation, I reached down to wipe and I couldn't find my butthole. I'm not kidding you.

"What the hell is going on here?" I asked, as I realized it had actually moved three inches north.

I know you're thinking, *This is* _way_ *too much information,* but I had to share it, because when does somebody have this happen? I knew it gave me a good laugh, and I hope it gave you one, too.

When I went for one of my early follow-up exams with Dr. Zax, I told him, "I love you. Thanks for my new boobs and my new 'v,' but I have to tell you, I needed a road map to find where I poop."

Well, he almost fell off his chair because he was roaring with laughter. That was a first for him!

✪

I did experience a few serious moments along with the hilarity of all this. Like I said earlier, I had to mentally prepare myself to let go of all that skin, because it had been part of me for such a long time. It was almost as if that outer layer was the very last bit of armor I had on me. It was all I had left of "the old me." But the best part of the old me resides in my mind—the flab was just excess baggage that had to go. My old skin was like a Laura Ashley dress from the '80s. It was comfortable to see it at times, but I really didn't want to wear it anymore.

To this day, I still get nostalgic for my former self, but not for long. There are so many discoveries to make with my new body . . . hell, I wonder where my belly button is these days?

✪ ✪ ✪

chapter *Nine*

Letting
Go of the
Past

$\mathcal{F}$inding my body parts was a cinch compared to figuring out what was going on inside my head. If only I could have had surgery on my brain, specifically in the part that handles self-esteem. Maybe they'll figure that one out someday—wouldn't that be great?

As I've said before, most weight-loss issues are much more emotional than physical. Losing weight is a symbol of shedding other things—like a hurtful past, current unhappiness, or any of the other issues that block us off from life.

Stripping away these layers along with the pounds was incredibly scary for me. My fat represented two things: (1) I really love food, and that will never change (nor does it have to if I'm careful with what I eat); and (2) I used food as a Band-Aid for bad feelings. In a strange way, piling up the pounds over the raw spots I had inside felt good because it was a routine—*my* routine—and I knew how to be the girl who found solace in food. It was like I could get a one-way trip back to Familiar Land, where I knew my way around, everything was the same, and the role I'd played for most of my life could be filled without much trouble. It's as if I stamped myself with the label FUNNY FAT GIRL.

Someone really smart (my mom) once explained it to me on a deeper level. She said that all of these labels are like karma in a way—we put our version of ourselves out there, and that's what gets thrown back in our faces.

I've come to find out that we don't have to be stuck with the labels we give ourselves. I used to say things like, "I'm meant to be heavy," so it was like a rubber band snapping in my face when my doctor told me that my weight was killing me. I got my wake-up call and thought, *What is this bullshit? No one and nothing is <u>meant</u> to be heavy, except for whales and really good crystal.*

When I looked deeper into why I believed that I was supposed to be heavy, I had to find the spot in my life where I first got this little emotional cart that I'd been lugging around my entire life.

You see, when I was a kid, even though my father loved me deeply, he had trouble expressing it. Mom, on the other hand, was always very supportive, sympathetic, nurturing, and loving. She'd always say, "Carnie, you can do whatever you set your mind to do." It was great conditioning on her part, but somehow my brain managed to shut out part of these words because I didn't think I was good enough to do whatever I wanted to do. I don't think I tell her this enough, but my mom is responsible for so much good in me. I hope she stops here and reads these words: *I love you from the bottom of my heart, and I'm so grateful for you. You gave me wings to fly, and a solid perch where I always felt I'd land safely. You're the reason why I'm such a go-getter, Mom.*

My mother was always so proud of me, but there was one area where she had deep concerns—my weight. It was so hard for her to watch me eat and eat. She tried to help me when I began to grow really large because she knew firsthand what it was like to battle a few pounds. But most of all, she was worried about my health.

My dad and I eventually became very close, and he was probably more excited and relieved than anyone when I told him I was having gastric-bypass surgery. To him, I'd like to say: *Thank you, too, Daddy. You're also a survivor who's been a great example for me, and I'm proud of us both.*

Anyway, after much soul-searching, I was actually able to visualize myself as a hurting little girl. I also saw a little boy standing next to me with a big red metal wagon. He was trailing around after me, putting my little hurts in his wagon like some incredibly handy best friend. When there wasn't any room left in the wagon, he began to pile my hurts up on top of each other, until they almost reached the clear blue sky. At which point, he said, "Carnie, we need to get rid of some of this stuff because it's much too heavy to lug around." I didn't listen and kept stacking on new hurts until the little boy finally told me with great sadness, "I just can't pull this anymore."

So I took over and began to pull this heavy load myself—but it was a real struggle to do so. When it got to be too much, I looked for distractions and parked my wagon in the kitchen. At least when I was eating, I didn't have to be pulling. But the fatter and fatter I got, it became apparent that the wagon wasn't the only thing I couldn't move. Pretty soon, I couldn't move *anything,* and I became stuck. That's when I had to choose between staying stuck or looking at my pile of hurts and getting rid of some of it. I understood that I *really* couldn't lug that wagon around anymore—it was going to kill me.

Now I can see that the real reason to lose weight is much deeper than I ever imagined. It's about letting go of the pain of the past, learning to live in the present, and respecting the idea of a hopeful future. Of course, it wasn't so easy to get to this point of enlightenment. For a long time, I was really freaked out. I felt like these kind of successes were usually reserved for people in Lifetime movies, not for me.

So after I lost the pounds, I started to feel my old instincts take over, and these weren't the positive ones. I'm talking about my tendency to take something really good and hurt it on purpose—sometimes without even knowing it. I figured that it was time to get some help with all this, especially when I found myself taking out pictures of me at my heaviest and really examining them.

My wonderful, darling husband (let's call him some nice adjectives because this story is heading south), Rob, was reading in bed late one night, and I was in my office obsessing over those old pictures. I was especially studying this side profile I'd taken the night before I had WLS. My transformation was so shocking that I still felt like I was in a fairy tale, and my godmother was going to show up and say, "You have to return your new body by midnight. Those new abs are just on loan. Ha-ha! It was all one big fantasy, so get out the size XXL T-shirts again."

In other words, I was having a really hard time dealing with all these changes, so I sat there and bawled my eyes out. Then I decided to drag Rob into my pain. See, this is why we promised each other "for better or worse" . . . because the worse was about to appear.

Rob was quietly reading his book, when I slapped down an old photo of me in my bra and underwear (also taken the night before my surgery). I never had the balls to show him these photos until this night—don't ask me why. Actually, I do know why now: They were horrific to me.

I waited for Rob to explain himself. I wanted him to tell me how he could have been attracted to me when I was that big. How could it be that he had the hots for me? How did he sleep with me when I was a size 28? No, what I really wanted him to say were the following words, in this exact order: "God, honey, you look so different now, and as much as I loved you then, I love you even more today. I'm so proud of you." (For the men reading this book, it might be a good time to write those words down because you could score big points one day by repeating them verbatim.)

Of course, men rarely speak "female," especially when we need it the most. It's still no excuse for how Rob glanced at that picture and uttered words that no guy should ever repeat to his significant other: "Jesus Christ! How could you do that to yourself? How did you let yourself get that big?!"

I sobbed, "*Whhhhaaaaatttt?* What do you mean? Thanks a lot!" And then I slammed the door and didn't speak to him for the better part of an entire day. Every woman knows this is totally rational behavior, right?

I went back to my office, and for about the millionth time in my life, I felt like a helpless little girl who didn't know what to do. In the old days, I would have been in the kitchen eating whatever was handy to soothe my pain. Better yet, I'd have been going through the drive-through (so I wouldn't be recognized) at the Dairy Queen, ordering a large Blizzard with extra Snickers in it. Now I'm strong enough not to do that anymore, but I'm still awfully good at crying and rage.

As I stared at those photos, I realized that the old Carnie didn't know any better but to let herself get that way—she didn't care enough to stop herself. But the new Carnie can feel sad and simply cry when she's in a bad mood, and that's totally healthy. She doesn't have to physically hurt herself with food. And I also realized that Rob was right, too: How *did* I let myself get that big? At that moment, I saw myself objectively, and it hit me hard.

Oh, yeah, Rob eventually did come upstairs with the "I-know-I'm-in-trouble" look.

"You really hurt my feelings," I said.

"Sometimes I'm afraid that you're going to get that way again. You know, let yourself go," Rob responded with such a soft, concerned look on his face that I knew he was worried about me—hell, I was worried about me, too.

"I'm never going to get like that again," I said. "No way."

He told me that he wasn't turned off by the old Carnie, but he *was* worried about her health and future. He told me that he wasn't crazy to have loved me back then, because he still loved that same girl now. You see, he peeled the onion of my personality a long time ago, I guess when I wasn't even looking.

I knew that acting out like this was a way to wallow in the past and resist feeling good. It was clearly time to get back into some serious therapy.

I told Marc, my therapist, about the photo incident: "I'm looking at these old pictures, and I don't really know who that person is. But I look in the mirror, and I don't know who *that* person is either. She just looks really different. I feel very torn."

What made my mind do flips was that I couldn't recognize my own face anymore. I knew I looked better, but my face just looked really different. It was so . . . narrow. I was constantly looking in the mirror, but it wasn't like the old days when I'd stand there, suck in my cheeks, and put my hands under my jaw to cover up my double chins, imagining what I'd look like thin. Now I *was* thin. It was kind of like living all my life in tropical weather and suddenly being plunked down into an Alaskan winter. I was sort of lost in new territory.

That's when Marc put it all in perspective. "What do you feel when you look at those old pictures?" he gently asked.

I blurted out, "I'm just so scared for her."

"Do you think you still feel a connection to her?" he asked.

"No, not at all," I replied. "I just feel sorry for her."

"Then this is the time you need to start thinking about mourning her and waving good-bye, because this is where the mental part of your journey is about to begin," he said.

I grabbed a wad of Kleenex and filled it with tears.

"You have to mentally let go of the past, that big body, and that person who lived in that exterior," Marc went on. "You can still feel similarities to her. And you can remember her vulnerabilities, too."

It was like a bell went off in my mind. I realized that I *could* let go of a certain part of me—especially the part I didn't like. It was all my choice, but deep down I knew that if I wanted to keep the weight off, I'd have to accept that I'd changed *and that was okay.* So I needed to say good-bye to all those unhealthy parts of myself. The good news is that I'd have an exciting new journey ahead, which would consist of my learning to live with both the physical and emotional changes in my life.

Like Rob told me, "She's still you." And he added, "Only she's better now."

"I guess I can't ignore the old or new me," I told him. "There have always been two people fighting it out. I don't have to let the old girl go because I'll always be in contact with her the rest of my life. I have to stay in contact with the old Carnie but be a little bit afraid of her so I won't become her again. That's why I pulled out the photos, ya know? Deep down, I know I have to keep her alive in my heart because she's the core of me. I don't want to lose her completely, but I don't want to be her again either."

For a long time, I was trying to balance both the old and new me, which was quite a juggling act. It was almost like I was on a teeter-totter, and I was standing directly in the middle, uncomfortable on either side. Finding the balance was going to be tricky, but I realized that balance is the ultimate gift in life, and it's what I work toward every single day. Knowing that I really could become a new person freed me, eased my mind, and opened so many doors emotionally, physically, and spiritually.

Isn't feeling balanced what it's all about? I just have to take the best parts of the old Carnie—her strength, her drive, and her fabulous use of some four-letter words—and meld her into this new person who has come out . . . a slut! No, just kidding! Why do I always have to throw in a joke when something gets heavy? (Okay, okay, I'll stop!)

★

Recently, another example of dealing with the past hit me in the kisser. Chynna, Wendy, and I were in the studio recording the new Wilson Phillips album. (I'll get into the reemergence of our group a little later. Yippee!) I looked at them both and said, "Isn't it cool that we've known each other for such a long time?"

Chynna laughed and added, "We've known each other so long that my daughter is now going to the same school that we went to when *we* were kids."

Zap! I found myself transported back to a very bad place—one that in the past would have been enough to make me go on a major binge. I saw our first-grade class, and what happened that could never be taken back. So the old, smart-ass Carnie went to cover up the hurt with her sense of humor. "Jesus, Chynna, please dig up some more really great stuff from the past," I joked in my most sarcastic voice.

"I know what you're thinking," Chynna said. And since she knows my past so well, she looked me right in the face and continued: "Do you remember us beating up on the red-haired girl?"

First, let me say that Chynna has the most amazing memory of anyone I've ever known. She remembers *everything,* including every detail of our childhood. It's truly a gift to have her in my life, because we can go into that scrapbook at a moment's notice.

Yet the minute she said the words "red-haired girl," I looked up in amazement because I hadn't forgotten her at all—in fact, I've dreamed of her many times.

She must be a symbol for all the mistakes I've made in the past, because when I think of how lucky I've been in my life, she's the one who brings me down to size. I'm not even kidding about this, because there have been nights when I've woken up with the image of this girl burned into my brain. And I'll be saying, "I'm so sorry. Please forgive me."

She was the girl I wanted to be in first grade. I was the fat girl, and she was the pretty girl with the milky-white skin and the luminous red hair. My envy of her turned to anger, because it wasn't fair that she was thin and beautiful. In fact, I wanted to hurt her so that she could experience some of the pain I felt, because I was certain that someone so exquisite never felt any pain. It's kinda funny, since this period of time was my first memory of being called "fatso" and being teased by the other kids. As I was busy making certain assumptions about the red-haired girl because of the way she looked, the other kids were doing the same thing to me.

These days it's almost like God doesn't want me to totally forget how cruel I was or that I'm capable of causing someone else to feel so bad, which is why I don't think He will allow me to let go of her. I wish I could find her and write her a letter to say "I'm sorry," which I know sounds ridiculous because now we're both in our 30s, and maybe she doesn't even remember what happened all those years ago.

This is the letter I write in my mind:

Dear Little Red-Haired Girl from the Santa Monica Montessori School:

It's been three decades since I've seen you, yet I still have memories of the playground at our school. I remember looking forward to recess so I could hang you upside down from the bars of the jungle gym. Sometimes I'd scratch and bite you until you began to cry. You were physically weak, and I was very powerful and strong even at age six. When you cried, I pretended that I didn't care, but deep down I did care. I was just too angry to know it. I was fat, and you were beautiful, which made me jealous. I didn't know what to do with my rage over how unfair this seemed to me, so I took it out on you. Other kids began to tease me for being fat, and I found the one person who was even more helpless than I was, because that's how much I didn't want to be the victim—or the only victim. I wanted to show the other kids that I wasn't the only one who could be hurt. I wanted someone else to hurt more than I did.

I just want to say that if I could take it all back and erase what I did, I'd do it in a heartbeat. I want to tell you that I hate myself for what I did. In fact, I have such a deep sorrow when I think of you that it brings me to my knees. I've thought about you for years, and I've even done some serious therapy to help me understand why I behaved the way I did in the old days. I wasn't mad at you, I was mad at myself—even as a little girl. I would never dream of hurting anyone now, and I feel so terrible about what I did to you, but I realize that I was an angry child who was really confused.

If I saw you now, I don't know if you'd tell me to go to hell or give me a hug. Whether you hate me forever or can find it in your heart to forgive me, I just want to tell you that what I did to you is among my deepest regrets. I am profoundly sorry.

Love,
Carnie

I know in my heart that saying "I'm sorry" to the red-haired girl isn't just about her. I'm also expressing my regret over so many things in the past, and in the process, releasing some of the guilt that caused me to weigh 300 pounds.

Although Chynna feels bad about this, too, she's able to put it all in its proper perspective: "We were kids. We didn't know any better. You have to let it go."

I wish it were that easy for me, and I admire the way Chynna can put things in their proper boxes. This memory should clearly be in storage, but it refuses to stay there for me. It's part of some of the deep pain that I've been working on for years.

I told Rob, "I blame myself for so many things. I feel like everything is always my fault. It's like a weird, senseless guilt trip I play on myself. It's nothing specific, and I don't necessarily even know where it comes from. Sometimes I just feel so sad, and I don't have anything to be sad about. Maybe that's why I wasn't good to myself for so many years."

Finally. There it was: my deepest secret.

Then I had a bit of an epiphany: "I guess if you have more days when you feel happy instead of sad, then you're doing okay."

These days, I like to look at my past as a big canvas. I scribbled some really hard and mean drawings way back then. But now I know if I see something I don't like on my canvas, I can erase it. The faint remnants of it are still there—after all, my memories will always be with me. I can never completely get rid of them, but I wouldn't want to. They made me who I am today, and they also made me strong.

In the end, I found that I can just draw over the bad memories and make the old pictures the background—it's the foreground that matters the most now. I can work on it and fix it, which, as it turns out, is something I'm very good at doing.

✪ ✪ ✪

chapter *Ten*

Ms. Fix-It

The other day I went to Borders and bought *Codependent No More: How to Stop Controlling Others and Start Caring for Yourself,* by Melody Beattie. It was a trip! This woman wrote the story of my life (ha-ha!).

I like to fix everyone's life, and the "fixees" react in the most interesting ways. For starters, my controlling ways drive Rob crazy because he's a very competent guy and certainly conducted his own life just fine before I came along. And for the record, my mother, sister, and friends, along with that nice guy who recently installed my closet shelves, can also call their own shots. (However, I really think that guy should make up with his estranged brother. Of course he didn't ask me for my advice, but I offered it anyway, and he took $10 off the bill.)

I've always been this way. Basically, my need to control others has helped me conveniently avoid my own issues, which I'd buried in a size-28 body. I was so busy fixing everyone else that I was too exhausted, drained, out of ideas, and depleted to even begin to delve into my own crap.

In October 2002, I was doing the fifth annual Carl Wilson Walk Against Cancer and Benefit Concert with my family. (I love that we're still keeping his memory alive.) There I was at the sound-check, rounding up the masses: "Come on, everybody. Let's go. Wendy, your makeup is perfect, so let's get onstage." Moments later: "I think we should start with this song." I could go on and on—and I did.

"Wendy," I asked my unsuspecting sister, "why do I always tell everybody what to do?"

"Why is the sun hot? Certain things are just givens," she replied.

"Oh," I said.

"You're a control freak," she said with a chuckle. It wasn't so much an accusation as a statement of fact, like saying I was a Taurus or something.

It dawned on me that I was still telling people what to do when I lectured on health issues at hospitals. I'm basically telling them what to eat, what to use as motivation, and so forth. Then I had another thought: I tried to control people even more when I had no power over myself. Now that I've developed quite a lot of self-control, why am I still captain of the SS *I Know Best?*

I've come to discover that I really *don't* know what's best for anyone else . . . at least not all of the time. Hell, you don't have to listen to me at all. I've learned that my way is only one way—other people are smart and strong and brave, and the way they do things works, too. When I look back at everyone who helped me get to my weight-loss goal, I know that I can learn so much from other people. Who would've thought?

Still, I get nuts when I think that my family members or friends are heading toward any kind of pain (there I go again, trying to control). I swear my concern comes from deep in my heart, but I also realize that people need to go through both good and bad things—that's life. After all, plenty of people told me throughout the years, "Don't eat that double chocolate-chocolate chip cookie or you'll gain weight," and I just did what I wanted anyway.

Back then I had all the answers. Yeah, right.

Nope, I don't have all the answers, especially when it comes to WLS. For instance, one day I strolled into a Lexus dealership to have my car serviced, and the cashier stared at me hard for a few minutes. Finally she said, "I just want you to know something: My cousin almost died because of you."

"Excuse me?" I asked, somewhat confused. "What? Oh, no!"

"She had the surgery because you did, and she's been in the hospital for almost a year," the cashier explained with some anger. "She had a bowel leakage, which turned into a massive infection, and it spread all over her body. She got pneumonia, and she almost didn't make it."

This was horrifying to me because just about every day, I was getting these great success stories from people I've helped or inspired. I was used to hearing, "Thank God, I saw that interview you did on *Good Morning America* because I researched the surgery, and I lost 250 pounds. Because of you, I can walk again."

This was the first time I'd heard something negative (other than "I can't keep my chicken down"), and it was beyond upsetting. I couldn't find any words to help this girl—I was devastated. All I could say was, "I'm so sorry! That's just awful. Is your cousin okay now?"

"Yeah, she's feeling much better now," said the cashier, "but it's been the worst experience of her life."

"Well, you know, it's pretty rare that this happens," I replied. (And that's the truth—it *is* a rare thing that an infection during WLS turns life-threatening.)

I went home that day feeling extremely bummed out, and I realized that I truly am having an effect on people's lives. That woman could have died, and I felt like it was my fault. However, I also knew that I can't fix someone else's life, their result after surgery, or their fate. Yet I was still feeling a pressure different from any I'd ever experienced in my life. That's when I knew what my role in the world was now. Inspiring others was going to be a job that I purposely took on, and it's now a part of me. However, I need to keep it all in perspective and know that I can't become too emotionally attached. When it comes to other people's struggles, I'm there for them, but only to a certain degree. The bottom line remains the same: *It's up to them*.

Later, I called my therapist, sobbing. "Not only do I have to take care of myself, but I also have to take care of everybody else." Images of the cashier's cousin kept flashing through my mind.

"Carnie, you can inspire people, you can motivate them, but you're not responsible for them," Marc replied. "You have to be able to distinguish that in your own mind."

This is still one of the most difficult things I deal with—I just can't be Ms. Fix-It for everyone.

★

As I said, I was used to a more positive vibe when it came to others who had WLS. In fact, early in 2002, I was at a hospital in Tulsa, talking with people who were thrilled with the results of their surgeries.

Of course, what I thought would be the high points of the trip didn't even come close to the reality. First, a woman who had lost 275 pounds (and who had been in an electric wheelchair for seven years) *ran* up to me to shake my hand and give me a hug. She gleefully said, "I don't know what's gotten into me since losing the weight, but I'm always running around like a spring chicken now." I think the Olympic judges would score her run back to her seat as a perfect 10; I know I did. She's a miracle.

And then something life-changing happened when I was signing books in the lobby of the hospital. A beautiful young woman named Becky approached me and placed a piece of paper and a photo in my hands. "Hi, Carnie. This is my mother," she said in the softest of southern drawls. "I don't want to say that Mama died, I'll just say that she took a visit to heaven."

At this point, I didn't know what to do first—hold this girl's hand, hug her, or tell her how sorry I was. It turns out I did all three. But what Becky really wanted was for me to read the piece of paper. As I glanced down at it, my eyes filled with tears—it was a death certificate, which read: "Death due to morbid obesity." Next, I looked carefully at the picture of Becky's mother, Jean. She was a lovely woman in her 50s with grayish hair and a sweet, round face—yet I could see how big she'd been. It turns out that she'd died of cardiac arrest.

Cardiac arrest stemming from chronic obesity is the number-two cause of death in women (smoking is number one). More than 20 percent of Americans are morbidly obese, so let's do the math: Four million people in our country are more than 100 pounds overweight and are suffering from a deadly disease. That's a staggering statistic. I'm not reaching all of them, not even close, but it doesn't stop me from wanting to make a difference. If Oprah can, I can. For that matter, we all can.

"As you can probably see from just lookin' at me, I'm more than 100 pounds overweight, and as much as I want to visit Mama up in heaven, I just keep thinking, *Not now. Someday— but not yet,*" Becky said, as she grabbed my hand and squeezed lightly.

"You're a beautiful girl—," I began, but Becky had more to get off her chest, so she politely interrupted me.

"I don't want to lay all my troubles on you," she said. And she looked at the floor when she quietly added, "It's just that watching somebody like you get to the other side with this thing makes me keep thinking that maybe I could do half as good."

We talked about therapy and her weight-loss options, and Becky told me that she'd had no idea that her mother was so seriously ill. "We knew she was heavy, of course, but we thought that someday she was gonna lose the weight. We hoped her breathing and sleeping problems would end." But Jean had run out of tomorrows, which is what happens in so many cases.

I looked into Becky's stressed-out, panic-stricken eyes, and watched her struggle for breath as she told her story. "I never thought I could do it either," I said. "But it's up to you to save your own life. You have to at least try. I'll do whatever I can to help you, and I'll pray for you." When Becky walked away, after carefully folding her mother's death certificate and picture and putting them back in her purse, I had to sit back and take a few deep breaths of my own. You never know after one of these encounters if what you said sunk in, but I felt as if Becky and I had really made a connection.

Later that day, I had the good fortune to meet Brandy, a 13-year-old girl who was 375 pounds when her parents decided that she should have gastric-bypass surgery. The minute I walked in her hospital room (the day after her surgery), I could see that the little girl was trapped in a shell that was so much bigger than what she should have had to carry around. Yet in her eyes I saw an exuberant, hopeful, positive child who reminded me of . . . me. She was just like me in the way she was resisting the reality of her size, but embracing life at the same time. And she had such a magnetic personality.

I knew she'd do well at weight loss because she wanted it so badly. "I'm so excited! I'm so excited!" she kept telling me.

"I know how you're feeling," I replied. "I understand how tired you are and that you're sore, but you're on this wonderful new path, Brandy. In fact, you're about to *run* down that path." When her eyes widened, I added, "I've been where you are—a little scared and a little anxious. Right now the most important thing you can do is to visualize yourself healing. I'm so happy for you. Your new life is just beginning."

I could see a shining little face inside those heavy cheeks, and even though she was groggy, her attitude radiated joy. "This is so cool!" she cried, trying to move away her tubes so I could sit down. "I can't believe you're here, and I'm meeting you."

Then she shared her dream to wear a regular-sized dress to her school's formal dance the following year.

"Brandy, I do this weird thing with my mind," I said. "I zap myself forward a year like a time machine, and I can actually see someone thinner. I'm looking at you a year from now, and you're so happy. You're in the prettiest pale pink dress, about to dance with the cutest boy in school."

"Really? You see me dancing, and my dress is pretty?"

"Honey," I said, holding her hand, *"you're* pretty."

★

Okay, back to my controlling nature. So what happens to a control freak who obviously can't control her own life at times. What to do?

Let's start with what *not* to do. . . .

For example, I *do* want to numb out at times, so I might have a glass of wine. Drinking wine is new for me, as I really didn't have a taste for it before my surgery. The recommended limit for a gastric-bypass patient is two alcoholic drinks per week. I have to admit that during a stressful week, I might have more than one glass of wine and a martini on the weekend. There's a part of me that wants to go out with my girlfriends, drink, dance, and party. But my therapist has warned me that with my type of addictive personality, I have to be very careful. Am I de-stressing with alcohol, or am I just having an occasional glass of wine with dinner?

I keep remembering how Leslie warned me that after WLS, quite a few people end up having problems with other addictions. It's called *cross-addictions*—people simply move from food to another substance to try to fill the void. This is something I have to pay attention to. So it's all about not being in denial and being honest with myself about my actions.

Of course, I could always just blame other people when things don't go right. Who can *I* blame for my ending up at 300 pounds? I used to blame my parents; I used to blame society; I used to find every excuse in the book for why I was the way I was. Guess what I've learned? Blame simply means not taking responsibility for your own actions. Now I blame *myself* for letting myself go. It's on me 100 percent for not paying enough attention to my health and body. As soon as I came to that conclusion, I could actually apologize to myself, and when I was sorry enough, I could change things for my own good.

I've been through enough therapy to know that it's too easy to point a finger at someone else in your life because they did this to you or they did that to you. In the end, you'll just resent yourself for resenting them, and you'll hurt *yourself* in the process.

I honestly believe that it's good to tell someone who's hurt you what they did. It then becomes their baggage and they have to live with it—it's not your package to cart around anymore. But after you tell them, then you need to find some forgiveness in your heart (if that's possible given the situation).

In my opinion, blame is just a cowardly shortcut to not dealing with your feelings and the people around you. You'll be surprised to see how cleansing it is to open up to someone who's hurt you before. Through many hours of therapy, I came to terms with my own blame issues. Now I know that the people in my life just did the best they could, and they were hurting from what other people had done to them. People aren't perfect, and we all make mistakes. In the end, it was up to me to forgive them and move on.

What should *you* do? Well, why not take a chance and blame yourself, or at least accept some of the responsibility? This isn't a bad thing because you might do something to get yourself out of a rut. You don't have to associate blame with something negative—you can put a positive twist on it.

Instead of my old tendency to blame my parents, I can also thank them. I thank my mom for teaching me how to take charge of my life. She also taught me difficult things such as how to embrace struggles and learn from them. These days it also makes me happy to know that I'm a lot like my dad. He's strong, sensitive, and funny, and I'd like to blame him (in the most happy way) for rubbing some of that off on me.

Again, maybe we should start *thanking* people instead of blaming them. Just a thought.

✪ ✪ ✪

chapter Eleven

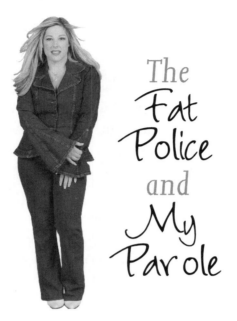

The
Fat
Police
and
My
Parole

*C*heck it out: Just when I'm thinking I'm thin, the feel-bad-about-yourself mafia pulls me back in.

I was totally furious when *The National Enquirer* called me *at home* awhile back (who the hell knows how they got my number) and said that their photo editor had some pictures of me where it looked like I'd gained some weight.

"Is it true?" the reporter asked in the sort of tone I'm sure they use when asking Lisa Marie Presley if she really ever slept with Michael Jackson.

"Is *what* true?" I replied, thinking, *Those assholes. I did gain ten pounds at one point, but I took it right off. And plus, I've been working out like a dog.*

"We hear that you're starting to gain your weight back," the reporter replied. "Are you worried about that?"

It turns out that they had this unflattering photo of me where I'm slumped over. Now we all know that this kind of posture can make it seem like we've gained weight even if we haven't. That's how we're designed, for God's sake!

"This is total bullshit," I said. "You have this bad shot of me, and it's so mean of you to print that I've gained weight." Deciding to appeal to this woman's humanity(?), I tried the honest approach: "Look," I said, "I've inspired a lot of people to lose weight, and printing this will be really depressing to them. They'll think I've failed, and that they're going to fail, too."

"We're printing it with or without your comments," she said, "so you might as well just tell us the truth." (The truth in tabloids? Ha!)

"You know what?" I said, reaching my breaking point. "I want you to find out if your photo editor wouldn't mind my coming to his house to take a picture of him on the toilet. I'm sure *he'll* be hunched over a bit, so it might also look like he's gained ten pounds, but he'll have to live with it."

"He probably wouldn't like that," the reporter answered, "but here's my phone number if you change your mind and want to talk to us." Click. *The Enquirer* hung up on *me!*

A week later, a man came to my door. "Are you Carnie Wilson?" he asked. "I'm looking for her." It was obviously another tabloid reporter, so I told him he had the wrong address and slammed the door in his face.

✪

Something strange also happened recently at a concert where I was performing with my family. For the first time in maybe forever, I didn't wear an outfit that covered my arms. I have the arms of a real person, which means that there's still a bit of flab still on them (despite all my working out and surgery).

Anyway, I was standing backstage at Royce Hall on the UCLA campus, looking at this strappy sundress I'd bought with the eyes of a rebel. *Fuck it. My shoulders and arms are looking so much better,* I thought. *Sure, there's still some flab on the underside, but who cares? I have the right to bare arms just like everyone else.*

So that night, I shimmied into my strappy dress and stood in front of a mirror with my arms at my side like one of those guards outside Buckingham Palace. Smooshing my arms into myself just made them appear bigger, but I didn't care—everyone said I looked great and I shouldn't worry about a thing.

On second glance, my black Spanish dress looked terrific, and my hair was long and blonde. I felt liberated because I don't think other people (besides Rob and my family members) have actually been in the presence of my naked arms in maybe two decades, let alone viewed them in a public setting. So I decided to just relax and enjoy myself.

The next night, I saw myself on *Entertainment Tonight*.

"Holy shit!" I screamed. My dress and my hair *did* look pretty damn good, but my arms looked terrible to me. "They're so big and flabby," I said, wincing. The actual TV segment, however, was very positive because it talked about how great I looked with my cool hair. In fact, the piece was called: "Carnie has fun, fun, fun as a skinny blonde!" *Skinny?* Ohhh, I love that word!

Feeling pretty good, I turned on my computer to do some work, but first I checked my e-mails. A guy I talk to on the Internet had sent me a message, so I read what he said.

Whammo—Fat Police, at your service!

"Dear Carnie," he wrote. "Saw the piece on 'ET.' You look a lot heavier than the last time I saw you. Of course, you still look great, but you looked bigger."

I started to feel a bit paranoid—worse yet, I went right back to that zone in my head where the old Carnie still lives. I began to see myself in my mind's eye as heavy again, but according to who? Howard Stern? I mean, he likes chicks bone thin. Speaking of bones, I felt my leg, which was leaner because of the muscle tone I was gaining from working out. *Can't this Internet guy see how my body is looking now?* I wondered. Then I realized that unless I invited him over for brunch tomorrow, the answer was a big, whopping no.

"Don't be so mean," I responded. "I've really been working out, and I'm feeling better than ever."

An hour later, he wrote back. "Well, maybe you haven't gained weight, but I could definitely see the flabbiness in your upper arms." Then he apologized and said, "But your hair did look fierce."

As I sat at the computer, I was really frustrated because it just wasn't fair. Imagine if you've been losing weight for two years, and someone ran up to you on the street and said, "Wow, you still look fat to me." It was totally demoralizing and depressing.

On top of this, *People* magazine ran a letter from a woman who had responded to a recent article about me. She said that I had my weight loss "handed to" me and there was "no effort" on my part. I read this while standing in an airport after a hospital lecture and I wanted to scream, "What a lie!"

I had to do something, so I looked up the woman's phone number in Minneapolis and called her up. I ended up leaving a message on her machine. (At least I hope it was her!) I told her that I was unhappy about the letter she wrote, and she had absolutely no idea what she was talking about because I'd never worked so hard for anything in my life. I reminded her that every day since I decided to have that operation has been an effort. Then I sweetly wished her good luck and said good-bye.

Damn it, this woman really pissed me off. I guess I still have to put the judgments of others aside, but that's really hard for me. There I go wanting to control what others say and think again!

But it *is* weird how so many people feel as if they can instantly critique my body now. I wondered why nobody wrote me to say, "Keep up the good work, you look great." Actually, some people *did* tell me those things, so why was I obsessing about the few negative comments? I really have to work on that one. . . .

Screw the Fat Police. I'm willing to take the hits because I want to reach out to others and tell my story. And I've recently discovered just how many people I'm helping. I always sort of knew I'd touch a lot of people in need, yet I never anticipated that there would be so many. However, when you understand that more than 55 percent of Americans are obese, that means that one out of two people can relate to what I have to say. I'm not reaching all of them, but I'm really trying to make a difference.

Others ask me about "going public." For example, I did a radio interview with a very sweet woman named Jane Ellen who works as a disc jockey in Tennessee. Just like me, she'd decided to have WLS and go through it with the world watching. She didn't have her surgery live over the Internet like I did, but she told her listeners what she'd be doing, so all of them were right there with her for the journey. I admire Jane Ellen because she wanted to reach out and show people that anyone can become healthy.

"Carnie, what do you think about my going public?" she asked.

"I think you're gonna be brilliant," I told her.

Times like those make me feel as if I've been paroled from the Fat Police. And getting back to that concert I mentioned a few pages ago, my own father didn't recognize the girl in the sleeveless dress with the long hair and the big smile. I could see him about to pass me by because certainly *I* wasn't the daughter he knew. When we were close enough to almost touch, Dad stopped in his tracks, did a double take, and then asked in a shocked voice, "Is that Carnie?"

I could have burst into tears of joy.

At that point, Wendy ran up, and Dad took both of us in his arms and said, "Oh my God! You both are so pretty. You're too pretty to look at."

When I was bigger, my mother always told me that I was pretty; Dad, on the other hand, refrained because he became so scared about my health. As I stood there backstage, I started thinking about the first time he'd told me I was beautiful, and I really got it.

It was a few months before my WLS. I was in Dad's backyard with his wife, Melinda, and my two little sisters, Daria and Delanie. I was sitting on the grass playing with the girls, when from out of nowhere, Dad looked at me and said, "My God, Carnie, you have the most beautiful face I've ever seen."

The way he said it was so honest, true, and full of love. He wasn't looking at my fat—he was looking into my soul. And in that moment, I got a feeling that I'd never felt completely before: total approval and love from my father.

I will always treasure that moment, and it really helped me begin to heal stuff with him. Dad can't hide his emotions, so you always know what he's thinking. I love that about him. I could see the pride in his eyes that day, and I saw it at the concert.

Later that night, I walked up to Eric Clapton (who was performing with us), and he gave me a kiss on the cheek. Jackson Browne did the same thing and told me I looked wonderful. But it was my dad, who kept gazing at me from across the stage with a look of such pure joy and admiration, that really set my soul flying. I wanted to take my bare arms and wrap them around him forever.

✪ ✪ ✪

chapter Twelve

Guys, Sex, and Weight

One day I was walking into a restaurant in L.A., and I noticed that guys were checking me out. I know that there are certain girls out there who are experts when it comes to being eye candy, but this was virgin territory for me, so I was a little freaked out.

A total GQ-type babe gave me the slow head-to-toe appraisal, which caused his girlfriend (who was a gorgeous skinny blonde) to lean closer to her man and then give him the type of death-ray stare that Jerry Hall gave Mick Jagger for decades. Women know what I'm talking about here. It was as if her eyes were two laser beams and she was drilling holes in his sorry skull. What I couldn't believe was that this blonde goddess in her tiny hip-hugger jeans was jealous of me! *Me!*

Then a few days later, a girlfriend asked me, "Carn, how are you dealing with more attention these days from guys?" Well, that's an easy one: I love it, and it's totally harmless because I'm married. However, I know that this subject can be a tough one for many women who lose a lot of weight. They can find all this new appreciation uncomfortable, especially if they're shy and don't care for the attention (never my problem!). But some women don't like the looks from men because they don't feel like their new, thinner selves. They can only see themselves as fat, so they wonder, *Why are guys checking me out? Is this some kind of cruel joke?*

My advice is simple: If you keep comparing your old self to your new self, then things are bound to get a little confusing. I don't care if you've lost 5 pounds or 500, it's important to really look at yourself *now*, in the present, and say, "I do look good."

Here's a typical complaint I hear from women who are uncomfortable with their new selves: "Ben never gave me a second look when I was fat, but he's practically stalking me now that I'm down five sizes."

Here's how I usually respond: "Sure, it's natural to feel a little angry and wonder, *Wasn't I good enough for you before, Ben?* But when you get past the anger, the truth is that you probably *do* look better without the weight, and you certainly must feel better—that's what Ben's really responding to. (It's only natural that he's checking out your butt, too.)"

✪

I personally never had problems in the guy department that I could blame on weight. I always had boyfriends, none of whom made me feel as if they were judging me because of my size. And I wasn't an exception—plenty of overweight women have great sex and wonderful relationships. I just knew that when I was in bed, I couldn't handle my belly hanging on the mattress and brushing those nice sheets. I'll stop right there.

I know I make a lot of jokes, and maybe that's to cover up the pain I still have keep deep inside. From first grade until I graduated high school, I was the fattest kid in my class. Sure, I was teased constantly by both sexes as a kid, but it wasn't like I was some poor, pathetic wallflower. I was really popular, and as the years went by, I felt less judged by my classmates, even the guys. And I've never been one to sit home on Friday and Saturday nights. I always enjoyed hanging with the guys.

I've also come to realize that we women have very different views on what's acceptable weight-wise than guys do. Allow me to translate:

1. Problem: A Bigger Ass

- *A man's view:* "A big butt is totally unacceptable unless it's on an African-American woman, my mommy, or Jennifer Lopez."

- *A woman's view:* "It's okay if my guy is a little chunky back there—and he'll probably be more accepting of *my* fat ass."

2. Problem: 20 Extra Pounds

- *A man's view:* "She's already this fat, and soon she'll weigh four million pounds. I should run for my life!"

- *A woman's view:* "I love a man who has that 'teddy-bear quality.'"

3. Problem: Bathing-Suit Season

- *A man's view:* "My favorite! We *are* talking about the *Sports Illustrated* swimsuit issue, right?"

- *A woman's view:* "Oh, what a nightmare. Can I just stay inside until October?"

4. Problem: Sex with a Pretty Face and a Fat Body, or an Ugly Face and a Great Figure?

- *A man's view:* "I need the body—I can always imagine her face as Pamela Anderson's."

- *A woman's view:* "I'd like the face *and* the bod, but a great personality doesn't hurt, too." (Boy, are we different!)

Some men, however, are true pigs when it comes to women and weight. This reminds me of what happened to a friend of mind when she went on a blind date. My friend, who's a size 12 and weighs 155 pounds (which is technically thinner than the majority of American women), met a professor over the phone who was very funny and sweet. They decided to get together at a bookstore for coffee, followed by a movie, 2.2 kids, and a house in the suburbs.

Casanova walked in the bookstore and looked around for a redhead, which was his clue that this was his blind date. He spotted my friend, who had taken two hours to get ready and made no less than five phone calls to girlfriends regarding what she should wear. Let's not even get into the centuries it took her to do her hair. Yes, she was a little excited about meeting this man.

Back at the bookstore, the professor made his first move. Instead of shaking hands to say hello, he greeted my friend by grabbing her upper arm and squeezing hard. Then he tossed out his opening line: "You're not thin. You're medium," he said, while finally letting go of her flesh. This was coming from a man who was 5'4", had a huge potbelly, little to no hair, and anchovy breath! He was also wearing an outdated jacket that was covered in dandruff flakes.

Later, when my friend called me in tears, I decided to cheer her up by telling her that if this Romeo had grabbed *my* arm fat,

I would have immediately touched his melon head, smiled sweetly, and said, "Not a large brain, but a medium one."

Men!

★ ★ ★

chapter Thirteen

The
Final Word
on Exercise

kay, I know I've been leading up to this part of the book for a while, so here goes. Can you believe I've actually written an entire chapter on exercise? But don't worry, it's not what you think. This is actually interesting! This is the part where I tell you that exercise got my head on straight. Please put down your cheese Danish for one second and stop hating my now-smaller guts.

If anyone had told me that exercise would eventually save me, I would have calmly taken a barbell and smashed it over his or her head. You see, for years I hated exercise for several very practical reasons, including the pain, the inconvenience and, of course, the sheer boredom it caused. I still managed to force myself to walk with my friend Lisa three days a week for many years. If only I'd been controlling my food at the same time, it might have worked. Instead, I eventually ditched the exercise and kept on eating. Great plan!

There was also a deeper explanation for why I refused to feel the burn: thongs. I hated all the women who wore those butt-floss torture outfits and then pranced around the gym like they were auditioning for "Riverdance." I used to wish that I could be some evil fairy godmother, go to the gyms of America with syringes of fat, and inject it into those toned asses. Then I'd force the little gym girls to drink milkshakes, sit back, and watch the cellulite grow.

Perhaps it's best to examine the root of my hatred for gyms, which really had nothing to do with workout gear. It all started during gym class in high school where I felt very fat, very inadequate, and very weak. I'd wonder if my mom could possibly write me another sick note for gym class—how many weeks a month can you have your period, anyway? Medically, I don't think three and a half weeks is possible, but I tried it.

Can you blame me? I certainly wasn't athletic, and I was never picked for teams. In fact, I'd actually hide behind this old oak tree when it was time to choose squads. Yet the real horror of my life was when the teacher would announce to the class, "We're testing you today on chin-ups, and then we'll match you up with the United States standard." Who knew there was a standard for chin-ups?

Why waste everyone's time? The answer was clear—I could never do a single chin-up, not unless there was a sudden change in the earth's gravitational pull. But there I'd be with my chubby fingers on the bar, trying to use my nonexistent arm muscles to hoist myself up for one actual second, and getting nowhere. I'll never forget Louanna (daughter of Lou) Rawls, because she could not only get herself up, but she could also hold herself there for a minute straight each time. It was another thing she had going for her—along with her incredible beauty, she was the freakin' chin-up champ!

To this day I can still remember that sick feeling in the pit of my stomach when the P.E. teacher would shake her head and announce in her booming voice: "None! No chin-ups. Put that in Carnie's permanent record." My, that was lovely.

Even after melting 150 pounds off my frame, I'm still not totally in love with exercise. Yeah, I know this is the part where I'm supposed to write that I experience a thrill when I look at a tread-mill and I've found spirituality in my own sweat. But let's get real.

Most mornings I'm tucked in my extremely cushy bed, think-ing, *I'm not sure if I can exercise because I have to wait for the water-meter reader to come, I have to take the dogs in for a shampoo, and I should balance my checkbook. Wait, is that Rob calling me? I certainly can't exercise if my husband needs me.* You get the idea.

I've discovered that the following tips are helpful when start-ing a workout regime that you actually plan to stick to for more than one week. I hope they'll help you, too.

Tip #1: Invest in cute clothing. It makes it so much easier when you're wearing something a size too small that sucks in your gut. Talk about motivation! Believe me, it works. Now if I could only look that way naked. . . .

Tip #2: Go to the gym—it won't kill you. For years I resisted exercise because I was sure I'd hurt myself and feel even worse. The truth was, it was such an effort for me to walk that I couldn't imagine working out, since I thought it would only put more pressure on my back and aching knee joints. The few times I tried to walk outdoors, it did hurt—which sort of pleased me because it was my "get-out-of-exercise" card. The truth is that careful and controlled movement when you're at a higher weight and, of course, under a doctor's supervision (I have to say that, so you don't sue me) actually does make your pain go away both physically and mentally. You also get to take lots of bubble baths to wash away the sweat, which is an extra "feel-good" perk in my book.

Tip #3: Find that exercise high (I'm not insane here). When I used to hear people talk about "getting high" off exercise, I thought that they were either high on something else or perhaps were P.E. teachers in a former life. In other words, this sounded extremely crazy to me. Well, one day I, Carnie Wilson, experienced something fabulous on a treadmill (of all places.) I started walking briskly, and then I even started doing a little baby jog. A few minutes later, I was actually running along and then I felt it. Some sort of chemical seemed to rush into my brain, and I felt like I was flying. *Whoa!* I thought. *Endorphins are a great thing.* (Now I know that running isn't so good for the organs, so I power walk. It's hard to resist jogging occasionally, though—those endorphins are powerful!)

I'd finally experienced the rush that all the workout freaks had been telling me about for years, and it felt really good. And I was burning 100 calories every ten minutes. The next day, I found myself wanting to work out, and then I actually became a bit addicted. Never in five lifetimes did I think I'd say those words. Now I plan my days around my workouts, which brings me to the next tip . . . please don't hate me for it.

Tip #4: Make working out your number-one priority after world peace. Each week I punch up my schedule on my Palm Pilot, and I figure out what hour each day I'll use to go to the gym. I make an appointment with myself to sweat, just like I'd schedule a voice-over audition or a doctor's appointment. Since life doesn't always go according to my schedule, I've told my agent and the people I work with that I can't do certain things until after my workout. I know myself—if I start making all kinds of excuses, I'll start slipping off my program and won't work out for days. Repeat after me: *Exercise is my job, and I have no choice but to get to work*. Getting fired from your own body ain't pretty.

Tip #5: Know that weight is a good thing. I'm not talking about what you find on the scale—I mean picking up those barbells in the gym. For most women, the real reason we don't lift weights is because that area of the gym tends to be filled with large men who don't have necks. When we girls wander in there, the first thing these guys always do is stare at our asses and boobs and then laugh at the little baby weights we grab off the shelf. Screw 'em. It helps to have a girlfriend (or a husband, in my case) and approach the weight room in pairs. Or just duck in, grab the weights you want, and take them to a more female-friendly part of the gym. You can also buy free weights rather cheaply and use them at home—but you actually have to *use* them. Don't put them in the corner of your bedroom to use as a way to keep your magazine pile from slipping.

I've never been so sore as I was when I began using weights, but I immediately saw results, which encouraged me to keep pushing on. I also recently read a study that said lifting weights burns fat all day long. Now *this* is the type of science news I can use!

Tip #6: Entertain murderous thoughts while exercising—it's okay. Don't tell the tabloids, but I'd love to shoot the guy who invented lunges. I also believe that the sadist who came up with squats should hang, and his death should be broadcasted live on the Oxygen or Lifetime cable channels. I know there would be record ratings.

Early on when I began to seriously exercise, I hired a trainer named Richard Giorla who tried to explain the principles of squats to me. "It's the best way to get rid of your thighs and tighten your rear end," he said in a breezy voice, and told me to think of it like sitting down on the john.

The only problem, I informed him, is that I don't repeatedly sit on the john and then stand up again—even if I forget to bring the cordless phone in there with me. And then I smiled at him and sweetly said, "You can shove those squats and lunges."

Richard instantly gave me the look that said, "Oh, she's gonna be high maintenance." Ignoring my protests, he started me out at about 30 squats and 30 lunges. This meant that the next day, I honestly couldn't walk. After two days of agony, he said, "Your conditioning is going well, and you'll be fine."

Thank you, Richard, because you were right—I now have leg muscles that I'd never seen before in my life. I didn't even know that legs had so many muscles.

Tip #7: Push it. Over my lifetime, I've gone to the gym many times and experienced no results thanks to my own effort (or lack thereof). I found it really easy to get in the car, drive a few miles, and go through the motions of working out. I could do a half-assed stomach crunch, or just collapse when the instructor told me to do ten more. If my cardio class was about to jog around the track, I'd conveniently have to pee and disappear for 15 min-utes. But I wasn't fooling anyone except myself.

These days I really push myself at the gym, to the point where I honestly believe I can't do any more. It's not that I hurt myself (see Tip #8), it's just so exciting to figure out how hard I can hit it because my body is often willing to go much farther than I ever thought it could.

Tip #8: But don't push yourself beyond reason. Remember to always listen to your body, because in those gung-ho days of starting an exercise program, you can permanently fuck yourself up. I remember doing those lunges, and my body screamed, "Attention, Carnie! This hurts! What the hell are you thinking? This isn't wimpy whining, but true, seeing-stars, wanting-to-die pain." I don't believe in suffering, so I told Richard, "My body is saying no." He understood, and showed me that there's always a different move to try that works the same muscle group. However, now he just shakes his head when I occasionally wimp out. He'll mumble, "Excuses, excuses . . ."

But don't be afraid to stop when you're feeling real pain. (That means that in the beginning I was stopping every five minutes.) I actually did hurt my knee doing those evil lunges. It healed, but it was a little scary—so cool it when you feel too much burn.

Tip #9: Talk to yourself. I've found that encouraging myself out loud really helps when I'm working out. On the treadmill, I'll say, "Thin, thin, thin," as I walk. And when I'm doing bicep curls with those eight-pound barbells, I'll look at my arms and say, "I'm gonna look so good in T-shirts this summer."

Richard has taught me to isolate (which, in layperson's terms, means "pick on") certain muscles while I'm working them, and I don't just look at them in my mind's eye—I verbally encourage them to be all they can be.

Tip #10: Expect the unexpected. I never expected to love exercise so much . . . even though there are still days where I wish that flopping on the couch and curling my knees into my chest could somehow be the latest Pilates move. Instead, I get up and try not to look at exercise as a chore. And Rob and I help each other with motivation. He'll look at me and say, "All right, honey, we gotta go." Or I'll tell him, "We can't flake on Richard."

I've learned that you have to embrace exercise, and dare I say, enjoy it. When I'm working out, there are moments where I'll just burst out laughing. Richard and Rob look at me like I'm crazy, but I feel like shouting, "Look at what I've done!" I'll think, *Thank you, God, for letting me be in the gym, and for the results.* I don't even hate those skinny girls in the thongs anymore. I mean, you really can't hate people for the way they were born, or make fun of their naturally bad fashion sense (tee-hee).

Sometimes I wish that all the people who talk about my surgery being "easy" could watch me in the gym as sweat pours down my face. Saying "I'll work out tomorrow" or "I'll eat better on Monday" while flipping the channel to the Food Network—that's easy. Now I have the best of both worlds—I watch the Food Network while I'm on the treadmill!

When I'm lifting weights on the bench press, I can't really believe that I'm the same girl who weighed more than 300 pounds a few years ago. My hands grip that iron, and it's truly a *Rocky* moment for me. Even better is when I run up a flight of stairs now, and I'm *excited* to race up them. That's a 180-degree change in terms of my mind-set. Before I started exercising, the mere sight of stairs threw me into a panic attack. *How am I going to get up those stairs and still be alive when I reach the top?* I'd worry. *How am I not going to have a heart attack?* Now I think, *Oh, stairs! Good calorie-burner.*

The other day I did *ten* chin-ups, and believe me, it was a victorious moment. Suddenly I realized, *You're getting so strong!*

I guess what I'm saying is that while I enjoy working out, I love, love, *love* the results of it even more. I also adore seeing my body change so much. In fact, I think of myself as a piece of clay—I'm sculpting myself into a different form, and my tools are found at the gym.

I still have days when I look in the mirror and see trouble spots, but most of the time I just mentally block them out and see a different picture. For instance, the other day I was getting out of the shower and I caught a glimpse of my naked upper bod in the mirror. I could actually see the definition in my shoulders and my upper arms. Later I went to put on a skirt and my thighs naturally flexed for a minute. I could see the actual muscles pushing through the skin. Of course I had to talk to them. I said, "You guys really make me proud."

⭐

That brings us to my workout plan. What works for me is walking for 40 minutes on the treadmill three to five days a week. I walk for about the first 13 minutes at around 4.0 miles per hour (zero to two percent incline depending on if I'm premenstrual or not), and then when I begin to feel the sweat dripping, I increase it to 4.2 and enjoy a brisk power walk. It's not that I keep such a close track on when to stroll and when to go faster. I just know when it's time because my endorphins kick in, and my body says, "Hit it, baby!" (It also helps to have Earth,

Wind & Fire's "September" on my headphones. That really gets me going, too.) The key is not to walk or run so fast that I feel like I want to keel over and die, but to "hit it hard," as Richard says. "It's the intensity of your workout that counts and the time you put in," he says.

I also lift weights for about half an hour three times a week, doing standard bicep curls, chest and leg presses, and tricep kickbacks that you can find in any weight-lifting manual. Then I work every single muscle group from head to toe once a week in a class called Cardio Barre. It's a new exercise craze in Los Angeles that Richard invented, and it's brilliant because it's no impact. We work on each muscle group by strengthening and lengthening them like they do in ballet classes. We even work out with a ballet barre that's attached to the wall, which teaches us balance. I've actually seen my ass rise from taking this class. (A lot of people have similar results from Pilates.)

Let's talk for another minute about pushing yourself. Yeah, I know you're saying that I have a *trainer* who pushes me, and that's true. Sue me. But you can be your own trainer and motivator, which is what I did for the first two years after my surgery. As Richard always tells me, "You're here three days a week—what you do with the rest of your time is up to you." These are words to live by for all areas of my life.

Anyway, my butt is really beginning to look good because I push it. The other day, I wore spandex pants . . . in public! Yes, I went to the grocery store wearing tight workout pants, a teeny workout top, and a big smile on my face (see Tip #1). I felt great, not like I was hauling around the island of Manhattan on my backside.

Of course, even in my spandex-shopping ensemble, I did pass the annoyingly reflective glass doors in the frozen-food aisles, only to note that broccoli was on sale but my arms still looked a little flabby. I guess you can't have everything.

But I couldn't help but be proud of what I saw.

★ ★ ★

chapter *Fourteen*

Playboy Part I: To Pose or Not to Pose?

Not long ago, something really incredible happened to me. A certain magazine called my manager, Mickey, who couldn't wait to tell me the news. "Carn, are you ready for this one?" he asked. "*Playboy* wants you."

"Shut the fuck up!" I shrieked. "You're lying!"

"No, I'm not," he replied. "Can you believe this?"

At the time this phone call took place, I was standing in the bathroom naked, and my hands started to shake so hard that I could barely hold on to the phone. Wait! I was naked and about to take a shower. Was that an omen? A *Playboy* omen?

Mickey went on to explain that *Playboy* wanted me to pose for a pictorial and to do an inspirational interview about my transformation. As usual, I asked him what he thought about the offer. "Obviously, this is huge," he said. "It's a definite career move, and a tremendous opportunity for you in many ways. I think it will be the best thing you ever do, but it's totally up to you. You've really gotta think about this one."

I reminded him that it was the worst possible timing, because I was about to do my reconstructive surgery: "Tell them that we can't even consider this until I have my surgery, and then I'll need some time to heal. I don't even know what my body's going to look like."

I was *dying* to hang up the phone and run into our backyard studio to tell Rob what had just happened. Picture my sweet husband on this average day, writing beautiful music and doing his thing—when I burst through the door, screaming, "You're not going to believe this, but *Playboy* called and they want me to pose. Can you believe it?"

I'm sure different husbands would have had a wide variety of reactions, but Rob jumped up and yelled, "Wow, baby! That's great!"

"Do you think I should do it?" I asked, even as I knew what he was going to say.

"Absolutely!" he exclaimed. "How many people get that chance?"

"But I'm scared," I whispered.

Rob grabbed my hand, looked deeply in my eyes, and said, "You gotta do it. This is great! You're beautiful, you should do it."

I was scared to death to put it mildly. I took 120 days to make a decision, because I had to think about it in terms of career and image. There were times when my mind said, *So many women have posed for Playboy and it did great things for their careers.* Then my next thought would be, *Can't I just take a few more years to decide?*

Women who take their clothes off in public have always amazed me. I knew you had to be pretty damn confident. Then it dawned on me that there was nothing tacky or raunchy about posing for *Playboy*. I realized it could actually be a very courageous move on my part. But I'd really have to own my own body to pose in *Playboy*—was I really ready to do that?

For four months, I went back and forth: *Yes, I will do it. No, I won't.* One night I cut out all the crap and got to the core issue: What would everyone think? Would my family freak out? Or what if I pulled up to the gas station one day and some buck-toothed teenager came out to wash my windows and said, "Saw you in *Playboy* . . . you've got a really hot ass!" Would I crawl back in my car and hide or give him a really big tip? It was all too much, so I finally decided to tell the magazine thanks, but no thanks.

And then, a mere 24 hours later, I was sitting in bed and some words came to me that made up my mind once and for all: *You're a risk taker, so what the hell? Take a risk.* Posing for *Playboy* felt like the ultimate challenge for someone who once weighed 300 pounds. It was like I was in this contest with myself and I'd won. So why not celebrate and invite everyone else to the party? I had the epiphany that this would be something that would either elevate my career or ruin it forever. Yet I really didn't care about that—something more important was at stake.

I realized that I didn't need to feel inhibited anymore—I *did* own my body. Maybe posing was just what I needed to finally feel free and completely liberated. Some women run marathons, some climb mountains or kayak across the deep blue sea, some jump out of planes and live to tell the story . . . I was going to jump out of my fears and pose nude for *Playboy*.

In my opinion, taking risks is the only way to move on to the next chapter of life. And I got a real kick when I imagined if someone had told me when I was 300 pounds, unhealthy, broke, and sad that I was going to be posing for *Playboy* in just a few years—I probably would have fainted.

Plus, has anyone ever been on the covers of *BBW (Big Beautiful Women)* and *Playboy* within five years? You gotta love the irony. It was cool to be an inspiration when I was heavy, and I was going to get to be an inspiration once more. I was even inspiring myself. I called my friend Leslie and said, "It wasn't that long ago that I couldn't stand naked in front of a mirror without being grossed out. Now I feel completely different. Maybe I *can* do this *Playboy* thing after all." Plus, what a great story I'd have for my grandchildren one day.

And then I called my mother. "I have an audition for a movie next week, we're starting my new book, and by the way, I'm going to pose for *Playboy*," I said. "Hey, how's your day going, Mom?"

After a few seconds, she slowly said, "I hope you get the part. Great, a new book. Could you please repeat the third one?"

"I'm going to pose for *Playboy*, Mom," I said proudly.

"WHAT!" she exploded, as I lifted my ear from the receiver. "Are you kidding me? I don't know about this, Carnie. Oh, boy! This is one you're really going to have to think about. My first reaction is that I don't have a good feeling about it."

I took a deep breath because I really did want to convince her why I'd made this decision. "It's like my final redemption, Mom," I said. "It's going to inspire women and show them that amazing things can happen to them, too." I desperately wanted her blessing, but then I came to the realization that whether she approved or not, it was ultimately my decision. She couldn't argue with that.

Of course someone else had a say in the matter, too—Rob. I walked into the living room and casually said, "Honey, do you want turkey burgers for dinner? Oh, okay, let's go out. And, by the way, the gas bill is due tomorrow, plus I'm definitely going to do *Playboy*. Should *I* make reservations for dinner or do *you* want to?"

Since Rob is one of the most understanding, supportive husbands on the entire planet, he said, "Do it! Honey, whatever you want to do, I'm all for it." (And then he made our dinner reservations. What a guy!)

I couldn't believe that he was being so nice about his wife showing her breasts, and possibly other body parts, to the public—not to mention to our family members, friends, and the 18-year-old kid who rents us stuff at Blockbuster. But he just said, "I think it's great. When will you get this opportunity again? It might even help your image because you won't be thought of as so clean-cut."

Clean-cut? I thought. *Me?!* I knew Rob must really be proud of me, yet I wondered how he'd feel when the magazine actually hit the newsstands. I couldn't believe that he was so secure, and I admired him for being that way.

Rob also has a great sense of humor. That night at dinner, he teased, "Are you sure you want those mashed potatoes? *Playboy,* honey."

I hit him with the menu.

★

Now that I'd made the decision, I found out that being in *Playboy* doesn't mean that you simply show up one day on a windswept beach in the Bahamas and drop your robe in the sand for some highly paid photographer. First I had to do a test shoot, which is like the toughest audition I'd ever had in my life. Tests with skirts and blouses are tough enough—naked testing was something else altogether, plus it required me to get a serious waxing. Now I really understand why they called it a "Playboy wax." I just never thought I'd actually be using it *for Playboy!* (As for the procedure itself, think of it this way: They just leave you with a landing strip, girls! But the pain is totally worth it).

Anyway, I had to take these shots because, even though several editors at the magazine might think I was great, it was ultimately up to Mr. Hugh Hefner himself to approve me. And that's when my real shoot for the magazine would take place. (For the record, I went into my test shoot thinking that Hugh would take one look at my pictures and cry, "Are you kidding?! Get me some girl named Bambi.")

I admit that I actually chickened out of the test shoot. Twice I insisted on rescheduling because I just didn't feel confident enough about my body. While I ducked my test shoot (it was like I was in the Playboy Bunnies' Witness Protection Program), I was obsessed with grilling everyone on whether I should pose or not. I guess I wanted everybody's approval and a pat on the back . . . but not everyone reacted that way.

I talked about it with my therapist, who was very encouraging. Marc felt that posing would be very liberating for me, because I was finally proud and comfortable with my body—not ashamed. He said that even though there would most likely be a mixed bag of reactions from people, I'd always been someone who takes chances. And judging from my past and how public I was with different things, I'd be strong enough to handle whatever I encountered. "They already judge you now," he reminded me.

I went back to my mom, who was still worried. I was frustrated with her reaction because I wanted her to say, "I'm really proud of you. This is fantastic." Instead she said, "I absolutely don't think you should do it. I think it's the wrong move for you. You'll regret it."

Afterwards, I naturally cried my eyes out from frustration because Mom's always been behind me no matter what. I called her later and said, "I won't regret these photos because I know I'll look great. Plus, *they* came to *me*—I didn't go knocking on their door. So I'm thinking of this as a major personal accomplishment."

Mom finally admitted that I had a point. She still wasn't happy with my choice, but she's always trusted my judgment, like I've trusted hers. This was just one of those things where we weren't going to see eye to eye on for now.

As for my sister, she didn't agree with my decision at all, but she did try some very good logic on me. "Women who pose nude are just looking for attention and want validation," she said.

"So what?" I replied. "Don't we all want attention and validation?"

Wendy agreed, but she still wasn't thrilled. "Well, maybe," she said, "but I don't see why you have to pose nude to get it." We had to see each other's point of views as separate and our own.

One of my best friends, Owen, said, "I'm worried about you doing this, and I don't think it's a very good idea."

I reminded her that the thought of being naked in public began years ago for me. "Remember when we were young and I used to flash our guy friends with my butt and my boobs? I wanted their approval even though they weren't going after my body because I was fat. It was my way of saying, 'I'm pretty, too.' I know they liked my personality and my openness about sex, but I never felt their acceptance. Now, sure, some acceptance might be nice, but who cares anymore? This is more about being liberated."

Owen told me that made sense.

"You know, I've never in my life felt this positive about my body," I continued. "I even told Rob that I'm tired of living under this banner that said, 'Don't look at me.' I *want* people to see me now."

And what woman wouldn't love to have those *Playboy* pictures when she's 96 and her boobs are touching the floor? Wouldn't that be the ultimate "remember when" memento?

It would also be my ultimate fuck you to everyone who had ever called me a fat cow. I knew I'd get a ton of reaction, but I didn't care. It would be my way of telling women out there that they could change their entire physical body, be the best they could be, and tell all their detractors, "Ha-ha!"

Weeks before I finally set a final date for the test, I had lunch with Marilyn Grabowski, then a senior photo editor at *Playboy*. Marilyn had been at the magazine for 40 years, and it was her idea in the first place to have me pose because she was so taken by my story. She said, "Carnie, I'm just touched by your whole life. Plus, I love your face."

Marilyn and I had a wonderful time, and we talked about body image and the way men feel about women. We also discussed what it would mean for me to be nude—I didn't want to titillate, I wanted to inspire. (Well, maybe tittle just a little!)

I had one other big concern. "Marilyn, I don't want to put down the magazine, but I know you guys cover up people's scars, stretch marks, and pimples. So you should know that I have an enormous scar across my belly from my surgery. Also, I'm not 20—I'm 34. I can only look so good and be so firm. So you're not getting perfection here."

She replied, "Carnie, this is all I do. I've seen them all. You have to trust me."

At that point, I dragged her into the ladies' room, pulled down my pants, and showed her my tummy and my breasts, which had been reconstructed a few months before.

She took a quick look and said, "You definitely need to have a little more time. I want you to lose ten pounds. But don't you worry about a damn thing—you're going to look great." She said this with a huge smile on her face. God bless Marilyn. She motivated me and made me feel fantastic.

I finally set a date for the test shoot and worked out like a complete maniac. In the same way that having a new boyfriend motivates you to go to the gym, the idea of a *Playboy* test shoot turned me into the female Arnold Schwarzenegger. For six months, I worked out every single day of the week. *Sweat* was my middle name. I pulled the reins really tight and got myself under the strictest of control in the gym . . . but I continued to eat and drink more than I should have. The whole thing was making me very, very nervous, and you know how I have a tendency to use food to make me feel "better." Uh-huh.

Come on, now. I had plenty to freak about when it came to this magazine. I was told that the average issue sells about three and a half million copies per month, and the third biggest-selling issue ever was one they'd done on weight issues. All those people staring at my naked self was enough to make me want to carbo-load and call it quits. However, I forced myself to cool it with the food and continue my workouts, and the results were stunning. My body was becoming tighter, harder, and in the best shape ever. Why is it that no one ever told me that the real way to lose those last stubborn ten pounds is to pose nude in a men's magazine? If this gets out, my neighbor will be Miss October.

As for me, I was Miss Nervous.

The Test Shoot

I arrived early in the morning with my dear friend Daniel Combs, who did the most beautiful plum eye makeup to go with the golden-blonde hair extensions my friend Tiara Jenkins had put in. They both deserve a plug because they're the best. Daniel sprayed my entire body with bisque-ivory base makeup from Fred Segal, to cover up my scars. I was still very paranoid about them, but not as freaked out as I was about the sexy positions the photographer was surely going to make me pose in.

For my sanity (and his own), Rob stayed home. Unfortunately, he didn't get to shake hands with Steve Wayda, my test photographer and a guy who knew exactly how to make a girl feel good. "You look great!" he said when I stepped into the studio. "Now let's figure out what to wear."

Next, Steve handed me a big glass of wine. (Thank God!) "They told me to get the most expensive merlot I could find," he said with a laugh.

"Do we have 100 bottles of it?" I joked. A few sips later, I was really loosened up—in fact, I felt like a little purring kitty. I was starting to feel very sensual and wished that Rob had stopped by for a quickie between shots. *Ooh la la!*

There was no time for any backstage nooky, however, because I was required on the set. They'd set up a big wooden sleigh bed for me with pretty white sheets and fluffy pillows—it was the type of bed you'd want on your honeymoon. I looked around at all the people in the room: including my friend Katrina; two lighting guys; Gretchen, the stylist; Daniel and his assistant, Sarah; Steve the photographer; and Marilyn.

I took a deep breath and asked them to put on an album by Sade to help me feel sexy. The first shot to be taken would be me in a sheer pink negligee (okay, it was totally see-through) with little flowery straps across the shoulders. But I wore a beautiful eggplant-colored satin robe over the nightie.

Steve asked me to get on the bed, turn on my side, and lean forward so we could do some cleavage shots. Moments later, they were on film, and soon Steve was showing me the Polaroids. "Look at this," he said.

I nearly fainted because I looked so good, and the shots were really stunning. The lighting was beautiful, my hair was perfect, my makeup to die for, and my chest looked like something you might order from a really good plastic surgeon.

"Now I want you to take off the robe," Steve said.

My heart began to pound as I pulled it off one shoulder. "I better look good, or Howard Stern is gonna rip me a new ass," I cracked.

"Okay, now expose your breast to me," Steve asked.

I took a deep breath and went for it. I magically relaxed and just let go of my inhibitions and internal fears. The minute my skin hit the air, I felt so excited and sexy. Before I could get self-conscious, Steve had me change positions. I took off the robe, got on my knees, clenched my fists to my tummy, and exposed both of my boobs.

Steve snapped away and then asked me to completely take off the negligee. It was the moment of truth, and I felt a little bit scared. But I swallowed hard, took it off, and got on the bed—placing a big pillow across my middle. I could hear Katrina softly crying in the distance. She looked so proud, probably because she'd lost more than 150 pounds herself.

Daniel came up to fix my hair and whispered, "This is it! Wait until you see these pictures."

I was really doing it! I was so proud of myself that I began to cry a little, which wasn't good for the makeup. I sat up and said, "Do you guys remember what I looked like a few years ago?"

The room went silent, and finally I heard Steve say, "Wow, yes, I do remember."

To break the seriousness of this moment, I offered up a bit of humor. I suddenly realized that my tampon string was tickling my thigh—they never warn you about this happening on the Tampax box! So I said, "Tell me you don't see my tampon string hanging out now!"

Everyone was hysterical. On the rag at *Playboy*—can you believe it?

Back in the dressing room, Marilyn gave me a big hug and said, "I told you this would be a life-changing experience." Then she explained that even though the shoot was amazing in her eyes, the photos had to be sent back to the Chicago office and then off to Hugh.

I became very scared that I might not make it. After all, there are lots of girls who do test shots who never make the real magazine. But I knew that I could at least tell myself I'd gone for it, and those photos would be among the most attractive ones of my life.

I asked Steve what he thought of the pictures. Did he think I'd make it to the real shoot?

He said, "I think you're in! Of course, we have to wait and see what they say in Chicago—but I wouldn't worry about it."

I started dancing around the room, singing, "I'm in! I'm in! I'm in!"

I waited a week for an answer and tried to put *Playboy* out of my mind, which wasn't easy. Finally, one morning while I was on my treadmill, Mickey called to say, "Congratulations, my dear. You're a Playmate."

I was stunned and couldn't say anything for a few minutes. He added, "Carnie, I'm so proud of you. In fact, I'm in awe of you. This is going to be the greatest, kid." Mickey is the best— he's taken great care of me from day one.

Naturally I couldn't wait to tell the most important person in my life, because his reaction was still everything.

When I came home with the test photos, Rob said he loved them, but I saw a little bit of fear in his eyes. I could almost hear his mind thinking, *Oh my God, this is my wife and she's going to be naked in Playboy. This is real.* Rob is *not* the jealous type; still, it took him a couple of hours to wind down to normal after seeing those shots, although he kept trying to make it like it was "no big deal."

Rob was sleeping when Mickey called, so I gently rubbed his arm and said, "Hey, sleepyhead. Your wife is a Playmate."

He held me in a tight embrace and said, "Congratulations, honey! I'm so proud of you."

"I thought about you during every moment of those shots," I said. "I felt sexier and prettier than I ever had in my life because of you, and you can see it on my face. A few times I even whispered, 'Rob, Rob, Rob. . .'"

He smiled and said, "You did it, babe!" Then a beat passed and he looked concerned. "Who did you say was in the room when you took these pictures?"

"Aw, honey," I said, "it was just me, the photographer, his two assistants, two lighting guys, two wardrobe people, Daniel, Sarah, Katrina, and—"

"Stop!" he interrupted me. "I don't want to know who else!"

✪ ✪ ✪

chapter Fifteen

Playboy
Part II:
Does Anyone Else Feel a Draft in Here?

For anyone who's ever wondered what it's like to shoot a layout for *Playboy,* allow me to reveal all—pun intended. I kept a detailed diary during the four days I stood buck-naked in a cold studio wondering if I looked a little puffy from eating pizza three months ago. Did I see a pimple forming? And was that pillow big enough to hide the things that would make my mother faint? My God, would the worries ever end? Anyway, here we go . . .

9 A.M., THE DAY BEFORE THE SHOOT: There was never a moment in my childhood when Mom sat me down to explain how to act the day before I officially posed for *Playboy.* I'm sure that's why I was such a royal bitch to everyone around me. Call it *"Playboy*

Mañana Syndrome" (P.M.S.)! I prayed, paced, and tried to yell at anyone in my sight. Someone suggested eating a few nuts. Yeah, that's just what I needed: gas at the shoot.

Noon: "You should keep busy," my friend Katrina said, but I couldn't stop thinking about my hair, my makeup, my thighs. Finally, I agreed to meet her at the only place a girl should hang out the day before her *Playboy* shoot—no, not at the mansion with Hugh—I'm talking about Victoria's Secret.

As Katrina and I were in the dressing room, trying on all these racy, lacy numbers, I realized that it was good to get myself ready for the feeling of lingerie, which is one of the best parts of being a girl. You get that slinky-cat, sexual, I'm-turning-my-partner-on feeling. As we tried on garter belts, bustiers, and bra-and-panty ensembles, we tried to keep quiet in the dressing room. God forbid we said "Playboy" and someone heard us—it was to remain a secret for a while.

Some 50 outfits later, I just felt exhausted, but I brought the most beautiful things home to try on for Rob. Let's just say that there were fringe benefits to this whole thing for him, too. You should have seen the smile on his face.

That Night: After Rob and I made love, I could hardly sleep. Can you blame me?

✪

7 A.M., DAY ONE: The alarm went off, and I briefly had visions of my *Playboy* shoot being like the one Cindy Crawford had done—on the beach, naked in a waterfall (where the water conveniently covered up the crotch shots), and so forth. I could also picture myself in a field of sunflowers in Italy. But then I remembered that Marilyn had said, "Carnie, there's nothing more beautiful than studio lighting and bedroom shots." She's no frickin' dummy, so I was sold.

When I arrived at the studio, I noticed that they'd been sweet enough to order me breakfast. I couldn't believe it. Food? At the *Playboy* shoot? I took one bite of my cheese omelette and bacon and prayed that I didn't get bloated.

8 A.M. TO 2 P.M.: My makeup and hair genius, Daniel; his assistant, Sarah; and I spent the next *six hours* getting me prepared, which meant major hair and makeup. It was so worth it, because each time I looked in the mirror, I felt like a princess. I was really glamorous—from my beautiful amber-colored eye shadow to the long, curly locks we'd created that made me look like some sort of naughty Disney heroine.

2:10 P.M.: After all that primping, I finally walked out onto the set, which had been built just for me in this huge warehouse-like space. I was reminded of the soundstages I'd shot music videos on, but this place had been transformed into a medieval castle—complete with velvet couches and chairs, old paintings, arches to stand under, and even a staircase!

I was really impressed, 'cause this was one major fantasy coming to life. To complete the package, they put me in this very tight corset.

Marilyn checked me out. "Can you pull this thing any tighter?"

"Do you want me to stop breathing?" I cheerfully asked.

"Trust me, darling, I know what I'm doing," she said.

So I sucked it in, cinched myself up, and then looked in the mirror. I never questioned Marilyn again.

I was reminded of the early days in Wilson Phillips. We made this one video when I weighed 250 pounds, and they put me in a suffocating belly corset to hide the fat and hopefully create a waist. The difference now was that I wasn't trying to hide *anything* because I looked amazing. And if *I'm* saying that I looked amazing, you know it must have been a pretty special thing, or else hell had frozen over—take your pick.

3 P.M.: It was finally time to pose, and I really wasn't that nervous for some strange reason. Each time a tiny doubt crossed my face, someone would say, "Oh, don't you worry—you're gonna look great. We all know what we're doing over here. This is a typical day for us at the office."

Breakfast. Boobies. It was their idea of punching a time clock, and I had to laugh.

4 P.M.: I began to think about the other women who had been in *Playboy* and how perfect their bodies seemed. I really couldn't help this, since the walls of the studio were lined with pictures of all the different Playmates—*life-sized* photos of these incredible women with extra-long legs and flat, world-class tummies. It was awfully intimidating. I hated their perfectly toned abs and arms. To make myself feel better, I decided that they must be total bitches with no friends. Then I was secretly thrilled when I noticed a stretch mark on Anna Nicole Smith's leg. Thank You, God!

I thought about my imperfect body and the fact that I could never look like these women. Then I glanced in one of the zillion mirrors around me and saw something different from the image I'd seen for most of my life: I saw a girl who was confident, playful, excited, and proud. I realized how lucky I was to be living out this fantasy. *Don't be negative,* I told myself. *You look hot! You're here for a reason—remember, they called you.*

6 P.M.: Back on the set, I had to contort my body into several often-painful positions. As I did my Cirque du Soleil moves, I thought of Rob and being seductive for him. I also thought about all those other women out there who wanted something for themselves and never went for it. I *was* going for it, and that made me really proud.

"This is for all the special women in the world," I told the crew. "This will also pay some bills for the next few years!"

7 P.M.: You wouldn't believe how much prep time goes into a major photo shoot—I don't care if your body and face have the dewy, pristine quality of an 18-year-old. We had to keep retouching my makeup so that my face and body skin would look radiant and even. Just the application of it was sort of funny. I mean, how can you feel comfortable when someone other than your significant other is rubbing makeup up and down your butt and inside your thighs, inches from your coochie?! I tried to ignore it when Daniel got to my inner-thigh area, but I'm so ticklish that I began to convulse with laughter, which made him laugh, too. God, I loved this day!

Not so great was sitting in the makeup chair for so long during a set-up change that my buns became totally numb. Man, it hurt. If I shifted to the right, I'd have a pain; if I shifted to the left, I moaned like an old lady. Ahh, the joy of posing for *Playboy!*

Meanwhile, my manager, Mickey, always has great ideas, so he suggested that I have a camera crew follow me around during the shoot. We did funny things and captured incredible moments. I can't believe how relaxed I was on the set. There were all these people looking at my almost-naked body, and I was *totally* comfortable with it. Honestly, it was way easier and much more mellow than I'd ever imagined.

⭐

8 A.M., DAY TWO: I was told that this would be the "challenging" day. This made me wonder if I was going to be posing naked and doing algebra at the same time. It turned out to be worse. Steve, my photographer, had me stand underneath a stone archway on my tippy-toes, arch my back, and turn toward him with my hips. I felt like a contortionist. On top of all this, I was supposed to look relaxed and sexy. The funny thing is that after I got everything in the right spot, I felt damn sexy. It was as if little bits of adrenaline and pleasure were running through my entire body.

"Relax, Carnie," Steve said. "Just feel the mood and get it into your body. Let your mind wander to wherever you want to go."

I instantly transported myself to Maui, standing with Rob on the beach at sunset (kiss, kiss, kiss . . .). I began to think about my womanhood, and I felt truly beautiful, like a goddess. I felt irresistible in a way I'd never felt before.

11 A.M.: "People are gonna flip when they see these pictures," I told Steve when he shared a few of the Polaroids with me. They were sexy, pretty, classically romantic, and just plain hot! It's every girl's fantasy to have a really gorgeous photograph taken of herself. Then I thought about how these pictures weren't just going to be for Rob and me—they were going to be for *everyone*. I started to hyperventilate a bit, but I was excited, too.

"What do you think, Carnie?" Steve asked. "Can you believe that's you?"

All I could say was, "AHHHHHHH!" because I was excited, hysterical, and scared at the same time. But more than anything, I was extremely proud of all the training I'd done with my body— all my hard work had really paid off. Of course the photos in the magazine will be retouched, like they always do with even the most perfect bodies. But I have the Polaroids, which *weren't* retouched, and I'd proudly show those to anybody. I was shocked at how good my body looked. Who *was* this girl?

More important, who would have thought that I'd ever be celebrating my body? I began feeling very honored that *Playboy* wanted me in their magazine. And I gave Marilyn Grabowski a mental hug.

10 P.M.: I collapsed into bed, horny as hell, with a huge grin on my face. Then I took that vacation with Rob for real. ♥

★

1 P.M., DAY THREE: My fucking right eye would *not* stop tearing. This had gone on all day long, nonstop. It was unbelievable! Daniel and I were going out of our minds because we'd spent seven hours on my hair and makeup. In between each roll of film that was shot (and there were at least 100), Daniel would come over to me, we'd laugh, and he'd wipe my eye and reapply my makeup. Both of us wished the day was over. I wanted to scream, but I was afraid I'd wreck my lipstick.

Somehow we managed to hang in there. I'll always treasure the fact that Daniel experienced this with me. He's a perfectionist, a professional, and a really great friend (obviously!).

1:30 P.M.: Exhausted beyond belief, I needed a little pick-me-up to help me make it through this grueling day. That's when Marilyn arrived, bringing me some of the actual photos and a strong cappuccino. "Come take a look at this," she said.

I rushed into Steve's office, where he had some of the photos up on his computer screen.

"Look at yourself," he said.

For a minute, I honestly thought I was looking at another person. *"No!* That isn't *me!* No way!" I cried. I looked about 20 years old, and even *I* started to get horny staring at myself.

Talk about instant gratification: prep, pose, expose, develop, and flip out. That's basically how it worked. Every so often we'd go through this drill as they showed me different pictures. What got me really excited is that *they* were so stoked about how I looked—this gave me the inspiration to take the next picture.

Steve even put six of the best photos on a couch in the hallway, while the film crew shot us talking about the results. "I want you to know that these are *not* retouched," he said. "Look, isn't that beautiful. Don't you love it?"

1:40 P.M.: I didn't care about a watering eye anymore—by now I was crying from joy because I'd remembered something.

The night before I had my gastric-bypass surgery, Wendy had said, "I want to take your picture."

I was in my bra and panties and had begged her, "Please don't look at me."

"Carn, how can I take a picture if I don't look at you?" my sister had asked in the warmest tone.

I cracked up because I realized that she was right. I'm actually laughing really hard in that picture, but some part of me worried that it might be the last photo of my life. You never know what's going to happen during major surgery. But three years later, here I was posing for *Playboy*. Talk about turning things around!

2:20 P.M.: Now the posing got *really* challenging. Steve had me leaning upside down on this really cool staircase that was created just for me. Next, I had to support my entire body on those stairs with just my wrists. "Throw your head back," Steve yelled, and suddenly I felt like a '40s glamour girl. It looked sexy, but I thought I was going to collapse. I thanked the Lord for Cardio Barre and pumping weights, because otherwise this move would have been impossible. I have to admit there were a few times, after a half hour of being in that position, when klutzy me totally lost her balance. Thank God the lighting guy was there to catch me. *Where* he caught me . . . well, that's another story.

Steve showed me the Polaroids of my poses on the stairs, and I gasped because I looked six feet tall, and my legs were so muscular and lean. *See, Richard?* I thought. *I <u>did</u> hit it hard!*

3 P.M.: I started to wonder how they come up with these positions and poses. Steve shoots women's bodies every single day, and he has 20 years of experience. All I can say is that he's totally fucking brilliant. He'd sit there looking at me—I mean, really examining me—and then he'd say, "Okay, move your body two inches to your right. Now turn your left leg toward your right, point one toe, lift your pelvis, reach long with your arms, and give me that face." Even though it often made no sense to me, as long as I knew that my body was looking pretty good, I could relax and get into the feeling of erotica.

4:15 P.M.: Billy, a guy from the magazine, wandered onto the set. Between shots, he said, "Carnie, this shoot reminds me of a romance novel." He was right—the setting *was* very romantic. The vibe was as if my husband was right about to walk over to the bed and make love to me.

I can't lie to you, though. A few times I felt a little tense about a pose, but I really only freaked out once. At that point, Daniel and Rebecca, the stylist, came over to talk to me. Rebecca, who had the prettiest blue eyes and the cutest shoes ever, said, "I'm 115 pounds and I feel just as insecure as you do. I'd *never* be able to do what you're doing right now. You're brave as hell!"

Then I looked at Daniel's smiling face as he gently pushed a curl away from my eyes. I took a deep breath, smiled, and felt loose again.

SOMETIME LATER: Steve got an emergency call saying he was needed at home. "You're done for the day," he announced, and quickly left. At that point, I was asked if I'd be willing to come in for one more day of shooting: "We want to shoot you for the cover."

I was speechless.

THAT NIGHT: When I got home, I did my usual routine of washing my face and trying to remove all the eyelashes Daniel seemed to have put on with cement. (I had to use mineral oil to get those suckers off—and lost a few "real" lashes with them!) Then I hopped into the bathtub and did a full-body scrubdown.

Rob helped with my back, and we talked about my day. I showed him the pictures the minute I walked into the door, and this time he was speechless.

After my bath, I got into my coziest pajamas and thick socks. So much for being a sexy mama—I just wanted to be comfortable. I sat in bed and studied my Polaroids, examining every part of myself. Then I grabbed an issue of *Bon Appétit* and looked up recipes for some rich, gooey desserts I could prepare for Thanksgiving. *Isn't this perfect?* I thought. *Here I am posing in* Playboy *and thinking about food. Surprise, surprise.*

I fell asleep thinking about sweet potato soufflé, but soon images of that tasty dish went away and my dreams took a more serious turn. I found myself looking at a friend who'd had breast surgery. She was showing me her right breast, but not her left. "Your scars are healing so nicely," I said. "Now turn around, and let me see your left boob." She hesitated, and I realized that her right breast was actually in the center of her chest, and her left one looked like an empty sac. She said, "The doctor's going to fix me up right away. I'm not worried about it."

Clutching my own breasts, I woke up a little out of breath. I thought hard about this dream as I stared into the darkness, and I decided that this one was very important and meaningful. I realized that my friend was actually me, and I was using my boobs as a way to show how "full" I am, yet I still feel "empty" on the inside. It's like all that posing and stripping had exposed these feelings. In a way, those photos took some of what I was in terms of my privacy. I was proud to show myself off, but I also felt as if I were giving away a part of me that I could never get back. I was worried that I'd ultimately be left with an empty sack.

I love the part of that dream where my friend said, "The doctor is going to fix it. I'm not worried." I think it means that I'm aware of how I can be empty inside, and I can use this feeling to take care of myself and continue to work on my emotions and insecurities when I feel this way. What a significant dream.

⭐

7 A.M., DAY FOUR: After three days, we finally got the hair and makeup down to a science—we were ready to shoot in three hours this time. My hair was blown straight, and my makeup was old-fashioned, movie-star glam. Women should know (and men, too) that *Playboy* isn't about boobs and coochies—it's about hair and makeup, period. Right, Daniel?

11 A.M.: Back on the set, Steve was prepping the location for my potential cover shot! (Once again, nothing's ever for sure until Hugh approves.) Each time someone mentioned the cover, I got more and more excited, but I quickly reminded myself that it was only a possibility.

I asked, "How do you see me on the cover?"

That's when Rebecca the stylist came in and said, "Carn, get this: You're doing the cover in an all-white Elvis costume. Take a look at this bra."

I was blown away, so all I could say was, "How great!"

Marilyn came in and said she wanted my hair to be straight, and Daniel suggested that we blow the fan on it while shooting. She agreed. "Playful and rock 'n' roll."

Noon: The vintage Elvis suit was skintight and open in the front, all the way down to my belly button. Hidden underneath were my perfect white lace bra and these funny (but fabulous) gel inserts to push my boobs up. I felt like I was wearing chicken cutlets over my nipples, which was good—no carbs in those babies! Rebecca even attached white tassels on the sleeves and stuck glitter dots in gold and silver all over the costume. My hair was perfect, and my makeup was strong yet soft.

The set for the cover shoot was all-white as well. They had a nice big bed with white sheets, and I loved it. *Click, click, click*— we took some Polaroids, and I could hear Marilyn and Steve whispering. I couldn't make out what they were saying, and it drove me nuts.

Finally, Marilyn said, "Let her see it." She brought me the picture and asked, "What do you think of this? *I* love it! There's your shot—modern, sexy, and fabulous!"

Then they handed me the Polaroid, which had a cardboard frame around it. In big black letters above my head, it read: *Playboy*. That was enough to send me into orbit. I looked sort of James Bondish in that picture: futuristic, beautiful, modern, young, and cool.

That photo was a mini version of the magazine, with my face and big cleavage on the cover. It was totally surreal.

"We're scanning these in to show them to headquarters in Chicago," Marilyn said.

"Okay," I said. Now I was getting nervous because this was serious.

"And then they'll go on to Hugh."

2 P.M.: An hour after taking a lunch break (even though I hardly ate a thing because I was afraid of looking puffy), I was rolling on a huge bed with an enormous headboard and gold satin sheets. Steve wanted me on my belly with my butt in the air. I liked this because I've always been proud of my butt—it was round and cute even when I was fat.

Rebecca draped this wonderful, romantic scarf with fringe all over my backside. I felt like I was in an oil painting on the wall of an old mansion . . . but the fringe was driving me nuts. It tickled my cheeks—the other cheeks!—and it broke the mood. I started to tense up.

"We can see that anxious look on your face," Steve said.

So there was only one solution. "Would someone bring me a shot of vodka?" I asked.

2:05 P.M.: Yep, that did the trick. "What the hell happened? Mama's back in the house!" Steve teased.

I guess that shot was all I needed to just forget and go off into Fantasyland again.

6 P.M.: Twenty rolls of film later, Steve smiled and said, "You're done. Girl, you did it!"

Everyone clapped, and I rewarded myself in my favorite way: I ate exactly three peanut M&Ms.

⭐

The Aftermath

Marilyn Grabowski called a few days later. Let me remind you that as photo editor, this woman has seen more tits and ass than Hugh Hefner himself. She's the one who told me that my shoot would be an inspiration to millions of women. "I just want you to know how proud we are of you," she said. "The photos are stunning, and we absolutely love you."

I asked her if I could come down to the office and see all the photos.

"We'll share them with you soon," she said. She also had this tidbit for me: "You know, there were certain people at the magazine (who shall remain nameless) who didn't want to do the shoot with you. They said you were more appropriate for *Cosmopolitan* or something. I really wanted to prove them wrong. And then the other day, one of these same people saw the mock layout and said, "I don't believe it. I love it.'"

A few nights later, Mickey came over to talk about what had happened and to try this delicious brisket that I'd made. (I love to cook for him.)

"Carnie, there are 20 million Americans who are size 28 and above," he said between bites. "A lot of women out there are going to be *very* interested in this *Playboy* piece, because from your surgery to your books to this magazine, there's never been such a high-profile person who's put it on the line in this way. No one's ever been this open." He added, "I think you're showing people what's possible."

Later that night, I took out the pictures of me at 300 pounds again, and I held them up right next to some of the *Playboy* Polaroids. Let me tell you, a lot of shit went through my head when I did this. One of the old photos is of me in a bathtub covering my breasts with this huge grin on my face; another is a really cute one of me standing in the middle of the room laughing hysterically; and another one shows me smiling and slowly taking off my shirt. Anyway, I'm wearing the same smile in those photos as I did in the *Playboy* shots. Even though I was 300 pounds, I never had a down spirit—I had a *scared* spirit because of the health risks, but I never let anything take that smile off my face.

And now that the *Playboy* issue is about to come out, I'm really excited (and yeah, a little bit scared, too). But one thing that made me so happy and calmed my fears was my mother's reaction to the final photos. As tears welled up in her eyes, she hugged me and said, "I'm so proud of you, baby. I can't believe you once weighed 300 pounds. You should be proud of these pictures, but more that that—you should be proud of what you've done for yourself."

Today I occasionally see a reminder of *Playboy* in my closet: the peach lace robe and purple corset. Hanging on beautiful wooden hangers, they're a monument to sexy mamas everywhere.

✪ ✪ ✪

chapter Sixteen

Welcome Back, Wilson Phillips

Speaking of hot mamas . . . Two months after my WLS, when I was trying to get smaller, something really big happened. My oldest friend and former band-mate, Chynna Phillips, decided to attend the second-annual benefit for my uncle Carl, who passed away in February of 1998. Billy Hinsche, Carl's brother-in-law, was the musical director for the show, and he approached me to inquire, "Do you think that Wilson Phillips would sing a song at the benefit?"

At the time, the group had been apart for eight years, so my answer was an honest, "Gosh, I don't know. All I can do is ask."

I called my sister, and of course her answer was, "I'd love to—absolutely yes."

Since I was obviously in, we just needed one more piece of the puzzle. I called Chynna up and said, "Jonah [my cousin] told me you're going to the benefit."

"Yeah, I can't wait," she said.

"Billy [Hinsche] asked if we'd sing a song." I said. "Maybe we could do 'Release Me'—what do you think?"

She said, "I don't know, Carn. It's been a really long time. Why don't we just see how we feel when we get there?"

The event was being held at the Calamigos Ranch in Malibu, California, and it was a beautiful crisp autumn day. Soon after Wendy and I arrived, Chynna came over with her sister Bijou. Chynna was pregnant with her first child, and she had the cutest round tummy. Thank the Lord—for once she had a belly!

Speaking of bellies, I'd lost 45 pounds at the time, and Chynna took one look at me and said, "Wow, you look great! I'm so happy for you."

I put my hands on her stomach and said, "I can't believe there's a baby in there." It was as if we were seven years old, and the world was our playground again.

Chynna said, "So are we gonna sing? We have to rehearse right now!"

It was just like the old days. People were taking pictures of us together, and I started to get that nervous-but-excited feeling about the three of us singing live together.

Moments later we went onstage to sing our hit song "Release Me." Billy had a great band, but he'd suggested that we sing a capella. What a great idea! The minute our voices began to mix together, the three of us got chills, and I believe that was the beginning of the reunion.

A few months passed, and Chynna called me up right after she gave birth to a little girl named Jameson. At the time I was living in Philly with Rob, trying to lose the weight and get on with my new life. When the phone rang in the middle of the day, I naturally thought, *If this is one more annoying telemarketer, I'm gonna lose it.*

"Hi, Carn," said the sweet voice on the other end.

I knew it was Chynna. "Oh my God! How's the baby?"

"Amazing! Everything's fine. We're so happy—and I know this might sound crazy, but I really miss singing with you guys. I was wondering if you and Wen want to start writing songs again and get back in the studio. What do you think?"

"Come on!" I screamed. "I've been asking you every single year to make a new album, and three days after you give birth, *now* you say you're ready?" I teased. "You're one of a kind!"

I got so excited that I started to cry. I told Chynna that I loved her and couldn't wait to meet the new baby. I also told her that I loved the idea of getting Wilson Phillips back together. Not to sound corny, but I heard our song "The Dream Is Still Alive" playing in my head.

After a few more minutes laughing and crying with Chynna, I hung up the phone and began to scream at the top of my lungs, *"Rob! Rob!"*

He ran upstairs, I'm sure thinking that I'd either fallen in the tub or had seen a really big bug. "Honey, what's the matter?" he asked.

I could barely get the words out of my mouth because I was jumping up and down. Rob looked so cute and concerned that I finally took his hand and got out these words in one coherent scream, "You're never gonna believe it!"

Even though he didn't know why I was so excited yet, he held hands and jumped around with me. "Chynna wants to make a new album!" I yelled.

I was fucking freaking out!

Next I speed-dialed Wendy, who at the time was falling madly in love with her future husband, Dan, a wonderful guy she'd met on the road with Al Jardine—Big Daddy Al, the matchmaker! I delivered the news in one big, excited gush of words.

"Oh, a new album," she said. "Really? That's great!" Her calm response was so typical of Wendy, but I knew she was really happy. Truthfully, I don't think she really believed it was going to happen.

No one will ever know how deeply I ached when Wilson Phillips broke up in 1992, but I secretly knew in my heart that one day we'd get back together. I just had to be patient for ten years.

During those years I often sat down to write a song. Halfway through, I'd be really excited about a certain harmony and think, *Wow, this would be a great Wilson Phillips song.* Then I'd feel a wave of disappointment and tell myself, *I guess it's not going to happen now, but maybe one day. . . .* Sometimes I'd even go into the recesses of my closet and find our old rehearsal tapes. There's a song on one of them that we wrote with Glen Ballard called "Love and Flames." I listened to it one day and felt in my bones that it could still be a huge hit.

On the day Chynna called me, I thought that maybe there was something about giving birth that had sparked something inside her. It was funny, endearing, and typically Chynna. However, at the time she was living in New York, happily married to her husband, Billy Baldwin, and of course, a new mom. We decided it wasn't exactly the right time to officially come back together, but that night planted a seed.

A few months later, we knew that getting Wilson Phillips back together was inevitable—and we'd make it work despite the fact that Wendy and I lived so far away from Chynna. We were going to get back together no matter what it took. So my closest confidant, sister, and best friend in the world (Wendy) and I flew out to New York, where we did some great shopping and started to work on songs for our new album in Chynna's apartment. It was like old times, and each time the three of us opened our mouths and sang together, we got those same chills.

It was also an interesting lesson for me. I had been so devastated when the group broke up that I needed to learn that if you just set something free, it truly does come back to you when you least expect it. And the rewards are so much sweeter.

In the spring of 2001, it was time to get really serious—we had to start writing with different songwriters and get our butts back into the studio. I'll never forget that first morning of recording the new album (which, by the way, is due out in 2004). The minute my eyes opened that morning, I was beyond excited.

I just couldn't wait to get to the studio and begin this new chapter of our lives.

I remember stepping out of my car in the parking lot of the recording studio, and I looked up to see Wen and Chynna. Arms around each other, we walked in as one. The entire girl gang. We were older, wiser, and sexier now, because we're just so much smarter, and ready to embrace second chances.

I know one thing for sure: The past can often be the sweetest part of the present.

✪ ✪ ✪

chapter Seventeen

The Final Course

Not long ago, I was in line at the grocery store when I saw a magazine story titled "Real People, Real Weight-Loss Stories." I have to admit that I felt a little awkward when I read it because I thought, *Wait a minute. I'm a real person. My story of weight loss is real.*

I was reminded of the time *People* magazine included my story in an article they called "Plastic Surgery Diaries." Needless to say, this title confused me because plastic surgery was the least of my struggles. Then things got even stranger when a woman came up to me at the Prescriptives counter at a department store. "Aren't you that Carnie whatever?" she asked. "You know, that Carnie something?"

"Yes. I'm Carnie *Wilson,* and I'm not a something, I'm a real person," I told her with a smile. (Did I need to pull out my driver's license again? Katrina and I still laugh about that to this day.)

On the inside, however, I felt really weird.

I think people's reaction to me and my WLS is very, very interesting. I guess I'll always have some explaining to do about it, whether I like it or not. And some people will never understand the magnitude of doing this type of surgery. Let me just say that I've never been more grateful for anything in my life, and I wish I could stand on a mountaintop and yell that out to people.

I'm shocked when people dis WLS. I mean, nothing is easy about having this surgery. It's work before the surgery, and then for the rest of your life it's even more work because you have to take extra-special care of your health and really pay attention to what you eat—*forever.* It takes tremendous work, attention, and effort. Believe me, there's nothing easy about it.

Yet, among its many rewards, WLS is usually fast, completely empowering, and like nothing I've ever experienced before. This country is obsessed with diets, and they clearly don't work. Surgery might be the only thing that will work for certain people to get rid of the weight and save their lives.

I sense a little hesitation and fear when some people talk about WLS. If only I had more time to drive my point home when I'm on TV—I wish Oprah would give me an hour to do so. But that's why I wrote another book. I wanted to let people know that there's hope. After all, that's what I see every single time I look in the mirror, and I want that for you, too.

I don't want you to think that WLS is something I'm *telling* you to do, but I'll always believe that surgery was the catalyst for all the positive changes in my life. It was like I opened a window, and now all of life's good things just sweetly flow toward me.

I'm no saint—I still have bad days. Am I perfect when it comes to handling my anger? Hell, no. Some days I feel like I'm invincible, and problems just bounce off me . . . other days are much more difficult. One day I might feel totally in control and make really good food choices, and the next I'm living in carb city and I may dump. The bottom line is that I'm a human being like everybody else, with the same actions or reactions.

For a long time, I didn't think that my life could change so drastically or that I could actually attain many of my goals. The two things I wanted most were to lose the weight and meet my soul mate. I can't believe that both happened in the same year. Today, we dream about going out on the road together. I can totally see him up there onstage wailing on his guitar and singing his heart out. We'd also ultimately like to have a child, or six, as Rob says. (Guess what, honey? You're helping me when it comes to changing all those diapers!) I never could have accomplished what I have without Rob's support, and I'm excited when I think of what fate has in store for us in the coming years. No matter what happens, we'll do it together.

Besides loving my husband, I love the three voices that Wilson Phillips's old producer Glen used to say "became one" when he heard us sing. I just can't wait for everyone to hear our new album!

As for me, it's totally my personality to have a million things going on at the same time. Who knows? I could start my own clothing line, produce records, or pull a 180 and do something totally different. Whatever—I'm always going to be a risk-taker and make things happen.

This book is meant to give you some inspiration and let you know that if great things could happen to me, then they can happen to you, too. Just remember what's most important: your health, your relationships, and the love you give out and take in.

★

Last night I had another dream. I was in the middle of the ocean, but I wasn't scared, because I wasn't alone—others were swimming next to me. My friend Tiffany stopped treading water to hand me a little bucket. "It's purified water, Carn," she said. "Pour it over yourself, and you'll feel good."

Looking into the bucket, I saw a snail, a little turtle, and a tadpole floating in there. "Wait a minute!" I cried. "Little slimy things are in there! *Eww,* I can't put this over my head."

So I tossed the contents of the bucket into the ocean, and suddenly all of the water around us turned black. I realized that in order to survive, I'd have to swim through the black water to shore—yet it was so dark that I didn't know what was below me. Strangely enough, I wasn't frightened. I just kept on pumping my arms and legs until I reached the white sandy beach, and collapsed on the shore. Yet I had a big smile on my face.

I realized that this dream had a deeper meaning for me. The turtle and snail represented the old, fat, slow-moving me, while the tadpole was my new self, which could move very quickly. A tadpole also transforms into a frog, which is symbolic—maybe I'm still getting to the point where I won't be afraid to take more leaps. The water was my fear of the unknown, or my new life. For a minute I wanted out of this ocean because I was scared, but some part of me also found the journey to be thrilling. I was eventually able to make it to the other side because I swam through my fear. If I just push myself hard enough when times are rough or challenging, I can get through it and wind up in a much better place.

It was also downright amazing because there was *no food in this dream!* If that's not progress, then I don't know what is. This doesn't mean that I don't want to continue dreaming, because just look at my life. It's a *living* dream, and my eyes are truly wide open now.

Am I finished? No way.

I'm still hungry for it all.

✪ ✪ ✪

✪ Epilogue

Sex vs. Chocolate

Of course I'll end this book talking about food and sex—two of my favorite topics.

Certain questions have perplexed humankind through the ages: How much is infinity? Where does the universe end? Is there life on other planets? Yet for me, the one question that will confound me for the rest of my life is: What's better, sex or chocolate?

Let's start with the similarities. Both are best when they're messy, both make your brain pop, and there's no substitute for either of them . . . although you *can* occasionally exchange one for the other. Hey, we've all done it. How many lonely evenings have we spent opening a box of Godiva as a substitute for foreplay or spooned with a pint of Ben & Jerry's and a big box of Kleenex?

Great lovemaking is about the perfect connection between two people, as well as the exploration of each other's bodies by making use of all the senses and sensations; while great chocolate is the perfect connection of ingredients, as well as the exploration of carbohydrates by making use of many of the best senses and sensations.

Chocolate is like sex for me because it makes my blood pressure spike, and afterwards I feel as if I could run up Mt. Everest.

I think this is what they call it a sugar rush, but I don't care for the clinical explanations—I just know that like sex, chocolate makes me feel hopeful, energized, comforted, and yes, horny. You might think I'm demented here, but I really do get horny when I eat chocolate. (Maybe someone should give me a contract as the anchorwoman of a new cable station: "Snickers After Dark.")

I'd go crazy without chocolate and sex because I feel that both are physical necessities that my body craves, and it takes sheer willpower to resist either. Rich, sweet, and silky in my mouth—I'm talking about chocolate here—what could taste better? I'm still talking about the chocolate. I savor every second . . . . now I'm not necessarily talking about chocolate!

I must admit that in my craving for everything and a lot of it, I often combine sex with chocolate, which is how my wonderful husband comes into the picture. You see, I often go to See's to buy Rob a little box of candy, which I hide in the back of my purse until I get home. I can't tell a lie. I also go there for a little "piece"—my free sample, of course.

I'll give that husband of mine my best sexy stare and whisper, "Honey, I have a little something for you." Then I'll perform a striptease that doesn't involve my clothing—little by little, I'll remove the ribbon from the box of candy, flinging it to the floor like a wild woman, then teasingly rip off the wrapping paper because now Rob can't wait, and finally, I'll open the perfect white box in the most agonizing, torturous way until I pop a sweet treat into the mouth of *my* sweet.

So what's better—sex or chocolate? My conclusion is that chocolate followed by sex, or vice versa, is the best-case scenario. In other words, have sex, and feed each other chocolate while you're doing it. (Don't knock it until you try it!)

As I wrote those words, my cool aunt Dee-Dee popped through my front door because we were going shopping. Since I've probably eaten ten pounds of candy with her in my lifetime (partners in calories), I decided to get a second opinion.

"What do you think, Auntie Dee-Dee?" I asked. "Sex or chocolate? What's better?"

She looked baffled for a moment. "Are you kidding? All I'm doing is eating chocolate because I'm not having sex!" she cried. "What do you think that means?"

"Auntie Dee-Dee, that's my next book," I said with a grin.

✪ ✪ ✪

Appendix

❂ How to Follow My Plan

A t least once a day, somebody comes up to me and asks, "So what do you eat now? Do you only eat this much?" at which point they make the A-OK sign with their hand.

I say, "Oh, no! I eat everything I want, but it's totally portion controlled."

The following plan illustrates what I mean. Even though it's helped me keep the weight off for more than three years now, it's also a great diet for *any* person who wants to lose weight. (**Note:** For gastric-bypass patients, the portions listed below are perfect. However, if you haven't had the surgery, you many want to increase the portions by a small amount. Check with your nutritionist for what's right for you.)

- **An hour before breakfast:** One or two cups of coffee with nondairy creamer or milk and two tea-spoons of raw sugar. I like Equal, but it's still full of chemicals. You might think that one packet a day won't hurt anything, but that's 365 packets per year! So I say just eat raw sugar. (If you like having your coffee with breakfast, go right ahead.)

- **Breakfast:** One egg (with the yolk) scrambled,
  poached, or fried in Pam or a teaspoon of olive oil.
  If you want, mix in a small handful of shredded
  mozzarella cheese; and sprinkle some salt, pepper,
  and onion powder in there, too. (One teaspoon of
  ketchup is optional.)

  Twice a week, I make my egg as usual, but then
  I add it to a small tortilla (corn or flour) with some
  fabulous salsa. A breakfast burrito! *Mmm* . . .

  (Also, take your vitamins now. It's good to have
  food in your stomach to avoid nausea.)

- **Water!**

- **Lunch:** One cup of the lettuce of your choice with
  three to five ounces of grilled salmon, chicken, or
  steak; three to five ounces of turkey breast; or a
  scoop of tuna. Sometimes I add little pieces of raw
  veggies such as carrots, celery, beets, and broccoli.
  My favorite dressing to use is Seven Seas Red Wine
  Vinaigrette. (If I'm out to lunch, I'll sometimes have
  a piece of bread with butter and a bite of dessert.)

- **Water!**

- **Snack:** I try not to, but if I have to eat a little something between meals, I'll have nuts, such as peanuts
  or almonds (sometimes mixed with raisins). We're

not talking about the whole can here, I mean a small handful. You can also have beef jerky, a little cottage cheese, a piece of string cheese, or a table-spoon of peanut butter (with half an apple or one small banana if you want).

- **Dinner:** Three to five ounces of beef, chicken, tofu, or fish. For example, I might eat six medium shrimp (either chilled with one or two tablespoons of cocktail sauce, or grilled on a bed of mixed greens drizzled with rice wine vinegar, salt, pepper, and olive oil). In addition, have a small serving of steamed, mixed veggies such as broccoli, carrots, cauliflower, or zucchini. Sometimes I squeeze lemon and melt a little mozzarella cheese on the veggies. I also have around two to four tablespoons to a half cup of a starch like mashed potatoes, baked pota-toes, or rice. If you're maintaining or haven't had WLS, your portion would be more like half a cup. (Nothing fried, and watch the sour cream if you have a baked potato.)

  And take your vitamins!

- **Dessert:** This should immediately follow dinner. Try half a cup of low-fat (or in my case, sugar- and fat-free) ice cream or frozen yogurt. You can cut up some fresh fruit to put on it—any kind of berry is delightful. Sometimes I crush a few almonds or peanuts and sprinkle them on top.

Or take two bites (and don't fill the whole fork) of any dessert of your choice.

- **Water!**

Special Notes:

I find that dining out is the area that can be the most tricky and semi-torturous, but you really can enjoy a healthy meal out—just stick to the plan. (When I see a menu, I want *everything!*)
Here are some other challenges you may encounter:

- **Bread:** Carbs are the devil! Weight loss equals no bread, maintaining means a half to one piece, and weight gain comes from two or more pieces. One piece of bread is the same, carb-wise, as a half of a bagel, half a cup of pasta, half a cup of rice, or one medium-sized tortilla.

  Believe me, carbs are the hardest thing to resist. If you can't say no, take an extra-long walk or do 50 sit-ups. In other words—make up for it, but don't beat yourself up.

- **Tortilla chips:** When it comes to chips at a Mexican restaurant, well, you really should avoid fried foods completely. If you can control yourself, then have one chip with a nice big bite of guacamole. The fat in avocados is actually good for you. After having WLS, it's possible for me to resist tortilla chips completely. Even though they still look and smell great, I just don't feel so good after I eat them. I used to eat two basketfuls of them! *Muchos tortillas es muy gorda.* Translation (I think): A lot of chips will make you fat.

- **French fries and potato chips:** Have one or two at the most. Think of them like a dessert—don't have a portion, have a taste. This is definitely one of the harder things to give up!

- **Pizza:** This is one of my favorite foods. Sure, it's not the *best* choice to have a piece of pizza for a meal, but once a week with a small salad is fine. Try to add chicken or some kind of meat on top so that you get a little bit of protein in.

- **Sushi:** My absolute favorite! I eat yellowtail, tuna, or halibut sashimi first. Then I'll have a few regular pieces of spicy tuna, spicy albacore, salmon, crab, or shrimp sushi. Rice really fills me up quickly, so I don't start out with miso soup (although it *is* very good for you—you could have a couple of sips of someone else's). Just remember that rice is a carb, and it expands in your tummy. You can eat less than you think and still become very full. (Also keep in mind that soy sauce is high in sodium.)

- **Salad dressings:** What's better than ranch dressing? Low fat is best, but it's all about portions.

- **Margarine:** Who knows what the hell is in that tub? I say use butter, but sparingly. And cook with olive oil, which is better for you and has a great flavor. The Italians know what they're doing!

- **Sodas:** Sugar sodas are out of the question, while diet sodas generally have tons of sodium. You should just learn to replace them with water or even iced tea. A couple of diet sodas a week is okay, but remember that you still have to drink your 64 ounces of water each day, no matter how many sodas you have. Fruit or any kind of juice is loaded with sugar. I dump from juice now, so I avoid it. Just watch the amount.

- **Alcohol:** Of course it's not really healthy, although there's evidence that one glass of red wine a few days a week can actually be beneficial to your heart.

    For people who have addictive personalities, it's very important to watch your intake. That would be me! I love wine with dinner, but I try to stick to just one glass. (**Note:** Gastric-bypass patients should turn to tip #64 in the next chapter.)

- **Special tip on carbs:** I don't deny myself foods such as lasagna, enchiladas, tostadas, and so forth. What I do is eat the protein first and then eat around the other stuff. I avoid fried shells completely. If I have a burrito, I'll take a few bites as normal, and then I'll open it up and start eating what's inside, eating less and less of the tortilla (the carbs).

  You can order meals without the carbs, too. For example, you can get a hamburger without the bun, or a tostada or taco salad without the shell. You can also ask your waiter for fruit instead of fries. Sometimes it's best not to have the temptation sitting in front of you at all.

- **Sugar/Desserts:** *Ahhhhhh!* My fave! What can I say? Don't deny yourself some dessert or chocolate, but just have a *taste*. Remember that desserts are loaded with carbs and fat. For people who are trying to lose weight and haven't had WLS, go ahead and eat a piece of pie or cake once a week, but don't have dessert on the other days.

  If you have the willpower, then do what I do: Have one to two bites of dessert at either lunch or dinner (or both) every single day. Then pour some salt over the rest of it. (It works for me!) Sugar is one of the hardest things to eliminate from the diet, and in the past, I became depressed if I didn't allow myself to have some. Why shouldn't we allow our-selves that kind of pleasure? I think sweets are deli-cious and very exciting to eat. The problem is when we eat *too much* of them. I'm now able to have a little and then stop. I get to really taste my dessert, love it, and appreciate it. I'm thankful for that one bite.

This kind of food will always be available to us, so we should get to indulge sometimes. On certain days they're harder to resist, and that's life.

(P.S. If you do indulge in a little pound cake, just remember one thing: Don't eat the leftovers out of the garbage—ha-ha!)

✪ ✪ ✪

● How to Be a Good Weight-Loss Surgery (WLS) Patient (If You Care)

This is a very special part of the book, because it's for those people thinking about having WLS (or who have had it already). I wanted to give you the most comprehensive guide possible for the entire process, from beginning to end. I learned the following things firsthand, and I hope they'll help you, too. (Of course these are my own personal thoughts and advice.)

1. Accept the fact that you're morbidly obese and have a potentially life-threatening disease. No more denial!

2. Admit that if you don't get rid of your excess body weight, you'll develop (if you haven't already) obesity-caused afflictions including high blood pressure, high cholesterol, heart disease, diabetes, certain cancers, sleep apnea, asthma, joint pain, back problems, headaches, gout, gallbladder disease, and circulation problems—including blood clots in your legs that can travel up to your heart and lungs and kill you. (All of this on top of the tremendous emotional pain being morbidly obese causes.)

3. Ask yourself how long you've been overweight. If it's been a long time, then you've probably tried to lose the weight over and over again. Be honest: Have you tried *everything* in your power, or have you just reached a point where you've given up and feel completely powerless?

4. Get your facts straight: Diets don't work for morbidly obese people. The cycle works like this: You'll go on a diet, lose some weight, but then gain it back (plus more). On and on it will go—you'll get fatter and fatter, and eventually you'll become seriously ill.

5. Recognize that morbid obesity is the second-most preventable death in the country besides the awful possibilities that can result from smoking. *How frickin' scary is that?* What an eye-opener!

6. Understand that WLS is the only successful weight-loss method that results in patients losing between 50 to 75 percent of their excess body weight. Only a small percentage of patients will gain back 25 percent of the weight they've lost. Think of all those people like myself who have lost 98 percent of their excess body weight. I've only gained back *five pounds.* Sure, I fluctuate with those five pounds, but I've never done that in my entire life. This has been more successful for me than any medical treatment or diet in history.

7. Surrender yourself. Accept that you need help that goes beyond going to a shrink or weekly Weight Watchers meetings.

8. But definitely get psychological help and start working on the issues that contribute to your disease. Address your need to stuff your feelings down with food, and work on self-esteem issues.

9. Research all the facts and information on the different kinds of WLS. Gastric-bypass (which is what I had) is the gold standard and the most successful. Learn about the risks during surgery and right after surgery, as well as the short- and long-term risks and side effects of all types of WLS.

10. Understand that the risks of not having surgery far exceed those of having it. This is a fact.

11. Confront your commitment. This is an extremely important thing to do. You need to ask yourself if you're ready, willing, and able to commit to the responsibilities that come along with surgery. There are several changes that you're going to have to incorporate into your life—are you prepared to do so?

12. Decide if the surgery is for you. If you're afraid of it, ashamed of it, or unwilling to accept it as a new part of your being, then it's not for you. But if you're ready for your body to finally become your friend (instead of the enemy), then you're on the right track.

13. Discuss it with your significant other, family members, and friends. Tell them about the surgery and give them all the facts, while also discussing the benefits and possible side effects. They need to know as much as you do to really understand and support you. However, if they've never had a weight problem, some of them might *never* understand your making the most important health decision of your life thus far. But I swear, after you've been successful, if they don't change their minds about WLS (I think they will) and notice your power, strength, and success, then they're just angry, negative people with their own problems.

14. Get over the fact that you need surgery to help you. You're weak and not weak at the same time, if that makes any sense. You've admitted that you're powerless and that you need help. You need a tool to get you going and to rid you of the afflictions threatening your health. It's *not* about giving in or giving up, it's about admitting that you're vulnerable to food and that you feel powerless. *That in itself is commendable.* Try to ignore the rumors and hearsay about WLS. It's not bad, and you're not a bad person. You're actually a brave, confident, courageous, and smart person, because you're taking control over your health and your life. It's the most precious gift you could ever give yourself. People won't always agree with what you do in life, but you've got to take command of your own life now and forever.

15. Accept that this is a radical thing to do. People close to you may feel excited, nervous, concerned, worried, and scared. That's okay—we have to let people express their take on the surgery, too. Letting the people around you express themselves and their opinions is a good thing. They need to feel like they're being heard, too, and that you're not just "jumping into it."

16. Respect other people's reactions, and let it go.

17. Do this for *you*. It's your life—no one can change you but you. Don't ever do something like WLS for anyone else. I know many people say that they do it for their kids or their loved ones, but I genuinely feel that you've got to do this for *you* and your health so that you'll be around to live a life with your kids and/or your loved ones. Inspiration and influences from others is great, though!

18. Give in to what you've denied yourself in the past—taking care of yourself. Just accept that you need help. After all, if a person with heart disease needed a valve replaced, would anyone even question it?

19. Prepare—this can actually be fun!

20. Research WLS over the Internet. Better yet, talk to people who have already had the surgery. These people are an amazing resource because they've been through it and can help answer some questions you might have. Talk to them and get their feedback when it comes to the whole experience. Learn from them.

21. Realize that everyone is different, from how they react to anesthesia, to how they heal, to how their mind-set is before and after surgery. And ultimately, everyone's different in their commitment. But we do have one thing in common: this disease called *obesity,* and the desire to become healthy.

22. Find a surgeon who's a member of the ASBS (American Society for Bariatric Surgery). *Do not* have just any gastric intestinal doctor or trauma surgeon operate on you. They might be amazing in their fields, but you want someone who only performs these surgeries to do your WLS. And make sure that your doctor has done hundreds of them. If you're looking into a laparoscopic procedure, then make sure that your surgeon has performed this operation at least 100 times. Look at his or her track record: If it takes four to six months to even get an appointment, well, maybe that's because the surgeon only does a limited amount of procedures. You shouldn't have to wait more than a few months for your surgery date.

Your surgeon should be confident, calm, experienced, and enthusiastic about your success, and should love what he or she does for people. You need to feel comfortable with him or her, and be able to ask every single question you can think of. You should feel a connection to your doctor, have confidence in this person, know that he or she feels that this is the best thing in the world for you, and be sure that you'll be taken care of. Tell your doctor that you want him or her to do a good job and to take good care of you. After all, it's your body. . . .

23. Make sure the surgery is covered by your insurance plan. It can be a challenge to get coverage with certain kinds of policies. *Don't give up!* Many surgeons will even work with you on this. It may take time, but then again, you didn't become morbidly obese overnight. You waited this long to change your life. It *will* happen.

24. Understand that any surgery is risky. During your WLS, things could go wrong. You could have a reaction to anesthesia; you could go into cardiac arrest (more of a risk for the super-morbidly obese); you could have a bowel obstruction, bowel leakage, or a hernia; you could form a blood clot in your leg and have it travel to your heart or lungs; you could die. Yes, you could die. But keep in mind that you could die having *any* type of surgery. The good news is that WLS is about as risky as having your gallbladder removed. People don't know that, so they think it's much worse.

The actual chance that you'll experience one or more of these problems is small. That's why you need to do research, and make ample preparations with your surgeon and the staff nurses at the hospital. You should receive extensive physical and psychological tests while preparing, which will determine if you qualify in the first place. These tests will help ensure that you'll be safe, and that you're the most prepared you can be. In addition, your doctor needs to know everything about your medical history, while the nurses can help you with more of the emotional and psychological components to the surgery.

25. Remind yourself that you've made a decision to improve your health and life. Accept the possible risks, address them, and then don't dwell on them anymore!

26. Stay positive. Go into surgery with an upbeat, positive vibe. Smile and talk to yourself—tell yourself that you'll be fine and you're gonna make this the best experience of your life. Positive people not only heal faster, they also have better results in the long run. So really try to keep your spirits up. It's normal to be scared and nervous, too. I was both.

27. Before the surgery, follow instructions from your surgeon. At the same time, go on with your daily life. Don't stop eating, but don't start pigging out either. Just do what you want. Many people start losing weight right before the surgery because they feel so excited about their decision. It's a relief and a fear all in one. But definitely *do* stop smoking.

28. Bring comfortable clothes, books, and anything that mellows you out for the recovery period. You'll be tired for a while, and you won't be running around for the first week.

29. Remember to smile and pray. It's a great combo. Good luck!

30. Know that you might feel uncomfortable and sore when you come out of surgery. It may feel like you've done a thousand sit-ups. You'll probably have a morphine drip, so don't worry too much about the pain. If everything's normal, you'll move on to Tylenol with codeine or a mild pain reliever for a few days to a week.

31. Walk, walk, walk! Listen to your nurses—if they tell you to get up and walk, then do it! The more you walk, the faster you'll heal. Breathe into the breathing apparatus, too. It's there for a reason. You don't want to develop pneumonia, so get those lungs goin'! This is crucial.

32. Follow all instructions. You might be given a manual or some type of pamphlet before and after surgery—read it and take its advice. Tell yourself that you want to be a good patient because you know it will make your experience better and more productive. You'll get certain medications, or specific instructions from your surgeon. Don't mess with any of this. The guidelines that have been given to you are there because you need them.

33. When you're allowed, start sipping that water, big time! You'll notice that it's like a little experiment every single time you drink or eat for a while. That's also part of the fun. Something might feel fine going down, or it might not, so take it easy. Don't gulp your water—sip it like a baby. Don't take big bites of food either. Take a pea-sized (or smaller) bite of anything you put into your mouth.

34. Understand that you probably won't be hungry. I wasn't for three months. I'd actually forget to eat—*the biggest miracle ever!*

35. If you fantasize about a big plate of mashed potatoes, a juicy steak, or whatever your favorite food is, that's normal. It's okay if you still want it, but remember one thing: You'll have it again. But your daily food plan will be strict and focused for now. This is to ensure your health and start good habits right from the beginning. The first six months after surgery will probably set you up for how you'll be eating for the rest of your life.

36. Realize that you might feel sad or even a little depressed after surgery. Anesthesia can make you feel out of it, tired, and can even change your perception. Also, those painkillers are just terrible. Sometimes they're necessary, but try avoiding them—yuck!

37. Go to support-group meetings, and share everything. You'll find that some people are having an easy time of it, while others are struggling—it's a good thing to experience it all at these group meetings. It will help you (and others) make it through.

38. Know that you won't be feeling like yourself for a while. You'll be a little off-kilter. Relax, take the time to heal, and know that it gets better every single day.

39. Start doing mental exercises. Envision yourself losing weight: Your pants are falling off, and you can run. You look at yourself in the mirror, and you see a difference—you also notice other people's reactions to your progress. You imagine yourself breathing better or not having to take your diabetes medication every day! You're proud of your control when it comes to food and how quickly you become full now.

40. When you eat, don't push it. Take small bites and chew slowly (but don't spend more than 20 minutes eating). Push the plate away as soon as you feel satisfied, but not full. Believe me, you'll understand what I mean—it's like a miracle.

41. Drink at least 64 ounces of water every single day. Remember that we pee out our fat. You should be urinating once an hour—every time you do, say, "I'm losing fat!" The more water you drink, the more you'll lose. However, try not to drink water for a half hour to an hour before and after a meal. You'll be really full from that water, and you need to get your protein in at every meal.

42. Remember that juice, coffee, iced tea, or any other liquid is *not* a substitute for water. I know that drinking water is a pain in the ass for most of us, but you just have to sip it all day long. Carry it wherever you go. Don't keep refilling your water bottles unless you wash them in hot water with soap first, as bacteria can form in there (gross!).

43. Watch out for your sensitive pouch. One out of three people will have some difficulty keeping food down, even liquids. Sometimes you'll find out the hard way about food "getting stuck." You might be taking too-big bites, or your tummy might just be really sensitive to whatever you put in it first. It *is* a healing wound. *Believe me, it gets better.* If you're having trouble, talk about it with your nurse or surgeon. However, if you're throwing up everything you eat for more than a week, you might have some scar tissue forming. Check with your surgeon *immediately.*

44. Don't feel like you have to eat three meals a day. You might only want one, or you might want two or three. Whatever you're comfortable with is good. Keep in mind that you need protein the most, and avoid snacking.

45. Take your vitamins (and get used to them, because you'll need to take them every single day for the rest of your life.) Taking vitamins is one of the keys to your survival now. Your body isn't absorbing all the nutrients you eat yet, plus you're eating less, so you're getting fewer vitamins and nutrients. You'll probably be supplementing your diet with a multivitamin, and vitamin B_{12} (see #46), calcium, and iron pills. Don't take your calcium and your iron at the same time, as they cancel each other out. Take your iron in the morning with breakfast, and your calcium with dinner or at bedtime. For additional absorption, taking 500 milligrams of vitamin C is recommended with your iron supplement. (**Note:** There are certain kinds of iron that you won't be able to absorb at all anymore—check with your doctor.)

There's a vitamin plan that I follow. I take VistaVitamins, which are the *only* vitamins formulated for gastric-bypass patients. The only thing I take in addition is a B_{12} sublingual (which means "under the tongue") from Trader Joe's once a week. I'll chew on a Viactiv once in a while, too. I found that taking my vitamins with food made it easier on my stomach.

Don't look at taking your vitamins as a chore—after all, you brush your teeth every day, right? You'll just need to learn how to work them into your daily life. Don't be embarrassed—be proud! People will be so impressed that you're taking care of yourself. And who knows? They might even follow your lead.

46. Remember your B$_{12}$—it's very important, especially during the first three months after surgery. This vitamin (along with protein) will help you with potential temporary hair loss/thinning. Don't worry if you lose some hair after three to six months. It's normal, and it will grow back. Understand that you can help this side effect by making sure that you get the *exact* amount of B$_{12}$ that your surgeon wants you to have, and by eating tons of protein. But be careful—too much B$_{12}$ can be very dangerous. Don't just take extra, check with your surgeon

47. Keep a food journal. You'll be able to chart your progress, as well as which foods you're incorporating into your diet. It's a trip!

48. Weigh yourself at least once a week. You can even weigh yourself once a day if you like. It's fun to see the scale finally becoming your friend. You may even get the urge to kiss it rather than throw it across the room!

49. Don't beat yourself up about things. Progress varies. Try to not compare yourself with others, but I know that's hard. Just remember that everyone eats and loses weight differently.

50. Follow these four rules, and I swear you'll get to your goal (or really close to it): (1) Eat your protein first at every meal. (2) Drink 64 ounces of water every day. (3) Don't snack between meals—I know it's hard as hell, but water will help you feel full. If you *do* snack, have a piece of beef jerky, nuts, cottage cheese, or a teaspoon of peanut butter—in other words, protein only. (4) Finally, exercise at least three to five days a week. You can do 30 minutes on the treadmill, take a nice long walk, join an exercise class, or go swimming. Of course you won't be able to do it all at first, but you can work your way up to it. The bottom line is that your new life will be about *moving* instead of sitting! It's so cool! And here's my bonus tip: Take those vitamins every single day!

51. Get into a routine and make it fun. Experiment with foods and cooking. Try to cook more so that you can see exactly what goes into certain dishes. You'll find which foods work best for you. For example, an egg and cheese for breakfast works great for me. Sometimes I dip it into a teaspoon of ketchup, but watch the sugar when you're first out of surgery. Even a small amount of ketchup could give you a dumping reaction. Whatever you do, do *not* make oatmeal, Cream of Wheat, or any type of carbs for breakfast. It's a bad way to start out the day. You need protein to keep you full—and you'll feel satisfied for hours.

52. Learn the facts about food. You might think that pea soup is a good choice for a meal because it goes down easily and is warm and comforting. But you're wrong—it's not the ultimate source of my favorite capital "P" (protein). Read labels and really know what's in your food.

53. Don't count calories—it's a total waste of time. After your surgery, you won't be eating the same amount of food or even enough calories to be concerned. Later on down the road, if you find that you're snacking more (bad!), then you'll need to pay closer attention. The simple fact is that if you eat more calories than you burn, you'll gain weight. Also, you probably have calories stored in your body that would last you an entire year, so don't worry about not eating enough.

54. Remember to focus on protein at *every* meal. Fill up on it first. Try to eat solid protein, but if you're having trouble keeping it down, talk to your surgeon about protein shakes or pureeing some bulk protein. There are many forms of protein you can try, including eggs, fish, chicken, turkey, beef, soy, tofu, cottage cheese, and beans. Oh, and FYI: Taco Bell's beans are refried in water instead of lard!

Remember that you can add salt, pepper, and different seasonings to make things taste good. I was so excited to try food after having the surgery, and it seemed like everything tasted so much better! I really savored and appreciated every bite so much more.

55. If you crave sugar or certain foods after a few months, that's normal. It's okay to try a few licks of a sucker or hard candy, which you can have at the end of dinner or lunch. Don't feel guilty about this! You should be able to have a bite of any dessert you want (but only at the right time!). Be careful about this, though—don't make the bites too big. Dumping isn't fun—however, it's my lifesaver now because I feel a certain reaction after I eat specific foods. If those foods are high in sugar or fat and I eat too much of them (which might only be two or three bites), I'll have a nasty reaction. The food will "dump" directly into my intestine, and my pancreas will be fooled and will produce a lot of insulin—it's like being a diabetic. I get cold sweats, my heart races, my nose runs and is stuffy, plus I feel like I need to barf, but I just can't. I also feel extremely tired and I have to lie down, no matter where I am. (Some people experience severe cramping and get the runs, too.) But the worst part is this feeling of impending doom that comes along with everything else.

This could go on from 15 to 45 minutes, as the degree of dumping varies. Sometimes I don't even know what caused it. You've got to be ready for the possibility of this happening. Believe me, you'll learn quickly what works and what doesn't for you. That's why I'm happy that I dump. Why would I want to be able to eat a lot of the foods that made me fat in the first place? I love being able to write that!

56. Don't be surprised if you start feeling a little bit different about your identity. If you do all the things I've been sharing with you, you'll definitely be losing weight—and probably fast, too. You may feel really uncomfortable about all of the sudden changes. *Don't worry.* It's part of the process, and a step forward when it comes to letting a more unhealthy part of you go. You'll also be inviting a happier, healthier self into your being.

57. Use whatever helps you adjust—support-group meetings, therapy, crying, rejoicing, or more exercise! Adjusting to your new self is a process that goes on for a year or two. As I write this, it's been three and a half years since my WLS, and I'm still getting used to the new me.

58. Be prepared for people to react in various ways to your physical and emotional transformation. It might even transform *them,* too. Remember that it helps to talk about how you're feeling and what the surgery has done for you. Some people might be proud, while others may be intimidated, since seeing someone succeed at something that they've always failed at can be shocking.

No matter how others react, you should be feeling very empowered after losing the weight, and your family and friends should be able to share that joy with you on some level. Remember to support *them,* too.

59. Have a blast with your new life! Your life will begin to really change now because you'll be able to do things that you've dreamed of doing for maybe forever. *Go for it!* Get on a bike, go in-line skating, dancing, bowling, skiing, hiking, or scream your lungs out on the highest roller coaster at the amusement park.

Now that you can fit in the seats at concerts or movie theaters, get out of the house. There's so much you can do now that perhaps you felt ashamed doing in the past or just couldn't physically do before. Celebrate the little things, like being able to run with your children in the park . . . or tie your shoes!

60. Remember, hitting a plateau is normal. If your weight loss starts to slow down after four, six, or eight months to a year after your surgery, then you're doing just fine. Now is when you need to be drinking more water, exercising more, and keeping the snacking down to a minimum. Remember that you're still losing inches, even if the *scale* is temporarily not moving. Don't let it get you down. Almost everyone goes through this—you'll get through it, too. But don't be in denial: Ask yourself, "Did I eat extra bread this week? Did I work out once or five times? Did I drink all my water?" There's *always* a reason why you've hit a plateau.

61. Eat more food now—it's okay. The "Golden Year" is over in terms of eating super-small amounts, so it's normal to find your intake increasing. And don't worry if you notice that it's easier to eat a bigger plate of salad than it is to eat a huge chicken breast. However, the solid, bulk protein will fill you up faster and keep you satisfied longer. If you think that you've "stretched out your pouch" because you're eating more, give yourself a little reality check. How much more are you *really* eating? What are you eating first at a meal? Sit down, eat a chicken breast or a piece of steak, and wait five minutes. I guarantee that you'll be totally satisfied.

62. Know that you can't really "stretch your pouch." But you can snack all day long and drink liquids during a meal—which will make it easier for food to pass through the connection of the stomach and the upper intestine. This means that food won't stay in your tummy as long, therefore leaving you not as full for not as long. So don't snack, and don't drink liquids during a meal or shortly thereafter.

63. Don't be threatened by holidays or special occasions. The good news is that your plan stays the same 365 days a year. If you *do* have more bites of candy, cake, or cookies, don't freak out. Just be careful, because it adds up. Increase your water throughout the day, and do extra exercise—it will really help.

64. Watch your alcohol intake. Two drinks per week is really the most you should have. Drinking isn't a healthy habit, and after you've had WLS surgery, your liver will be more sensitive. Be careful, because you can really feel the effects faster. Just watch it.

65. Call your surgeon if you have any physical problems including severe and persistant gas, nausea, and/or constipation (which usually comes from not drinking enough water); or a hernia. You need to deal with it right away.

66. Continue to follow the four rules I mentioned earlier, and you'll lose your weight and maintain it forever. However, it won't come without serious effort and commitment. Think about how long this list is when people question if WLS is "easy"! The fools!

67. Try to stop and recognize what you're doing if you start to revert to old habits. Watch your patterns—are you continuing to eat even though you're full? Whether you're one year or five years post-op, stop and talk to yourself! The worst thing you can do is ignore what's happening, for that's how the pounds will creep back. I was ten pounds up at one point, which was the result of snacking, too much wine, and not enough exercise. This reminded me that WLS is never a *cure* for our disease— it's just a helpful tool. Follow-up is the key to maintenance. (Support-group meetings are also helpful.)

68. Weigh yourself every morning at the same time when you reach the one-year post-op period, because it's a good way to see how your body fluctuates. Your weight depends on your salt and water intake, or that time of the month if you're a woman. Remember that it's easy to lose the weight, but it's easy to gain it back, too. Don't become obsessed with the scale, but keep it a big part of your life. It will keep you aware.

69. Make sure to have your blood work done every six months from now on. You need to keep an eye on your blood levels (especially your iron and calcium).

70. Get help if you're having emotional difficulty being a totally new person or are now addicted to other things such as alcohol or even drugs.

71. When it comes to having children, you should wait at least 12 to 18 months post-op to ensure both your and your baby's health. At this point, you'll be eating enough that your baby can grow healthy and strong. There's no negative effect on pregnancy after having WLS. In fact, you'll probably become more fertile because your hormones aren't out of whack. In addition, there's less of a chance of developing gestational diabetes, and you might experience a more pleasant pregnancy because you're not carrying around that additional weight.

72. Don't worry about your excess skin. It might not bother you at all, or it might totally gross you out. If it does, then it's certainly an option to have it removed. Try to get your insurance to cover some of it. You have rights in this area—fight for them!

73. Be a role model for others. Teach them what you've been through, what you've learned, and how it's changing you for the better. This is what I do, and it feels so good.

74. Take pride in your accomplishments, and don't let envious people get you down. People sometimes like to avoid their own problems by pointing the finger in someone else's direction. Remember how hard you've worked, and ignore negativity from others. I know it's not easy, but look at how far you've come. If you can do this, then you can handle *anything!*

75. Every day, for the rest of your life, thank God and honor your tool forever. Be grateful for this surgery, your willpower, and the strength you've welcomed into your life, because all of the above has made you as successful as you are now. Remember that you saved your life, and in turn, maybe you can help someone else save their life.

⭐

Congratulations, and remember my friend Pam's favorite slogan: "Progress, not perfection."

⭐ ⭐ ⭐

• About the Authors

Carnie Wilson is an author, actress, voice-over artist, singer, and motivator living in Los Angeles. In addition to running her own obesity support group at **Spotlighthealth.com**, she lectures monthly at various hospitals to large groups of people with whom she shares her personal story, and helps to educate them on morbid obesity. In her spare time, Carnie has a serious passion for cooking and tries out all her gourmet dishes on her adorable musician husband, Rob, while the leftovers are devoured by their three affectionate dogs. She still can't believe that a pair of Low-Rise Boot Cut jeans from the Gap in size six hangs in her closet. She's actually wearing them these days instead of just staring at them.

Also visit **www.carniewilson.com** for additional information, including Carnie's forthcoming solo CD due out in fall 2003.

✪ ✪ ✪

Cindy Pearlman is a nationally syndicated writer for the *New York Times Syndicate* and the *Chicago Sun-Times.* Her work has appeared in *Entertainment Weekly, Premiere, People, Ladies' Home Journal, McCall's, Seventeen, Movieline,* and *Cinescape.* Over the past 15 years, she has interviewed Hollywood's biggest stars, who appear in her column "The Big Picture." Cindy is also the co-author of *Simple Things* (with Jim Brickman), *It's Not about the Horse* (with Wyatt Webb), *Born Knowing* (with John Holland), and *Flex Ability* (with Flex Wheeler).

✪ ✪ ✪

Notes

Notes

Notes

Notes

Notes

✪ ✪ ✪

We hope you enjoyed this Hay House book.
If you would like to receive a free catalog featuring additional
Hay House books and products, or if you would like information
about the Hay Foundation, please contact:

Hay House, Inc.
P.O. Box 5100
Carlsbad, CA 92018-5100

(760) 431-7695 or **(800) 654-5126**
(760) 431-6948 (fax) or **(800) 650-5115 (fax)**
www.hayhouse.com

✪

Published and distributed in Australia by: Hay House Australia,
Ltd., 18/36 Ralph St., Alexandria NSW 2015 • *Phone:* 612-9669-4299
• *Fax:* 612-9669-4144 • www.hayhouse.com.au

Published and Distributed in the United Kingdom by:
Hay House UK, Ltd. • Unit 202, Canalot Studios •
222 Kensal Rd., London W10 5BN • *Phone:* 44-20-8962-1230 •
Fax: 44-20-8962-1239 • www.hayhouse.co.uk

Distributed in Canada by: Raincoast • 9050 Shaughnessy St.,
Vancouver, B.C. V6P 6E5 •
Phone: (604) 323-7100 • *Fax:* (604) 323-2600

✪ ✪ ✪

Sign up via the Hay House USA Website to receive the Hay House online newsletter
and stay informed about what's going on with your favorite authors. You'll receive
bimonthly announcements about: Discounts and Offers, Special Events, Product
Highlights, Free Excerpts, Giveaways, and more!